Your Divorce Support Team

250+ Questions to Help You Build Your Divorce Support Team

Genevieve "Jenny" Dreizen

Olivia Dreizen Howell

FIRST EDITION

This book was set in 10-14 pt. Times New Roman

by Fresh Starts Registry

ISBN 979-8-9881059-7-8

Published by Fresh Starts Registry

Distributed by Fresh Starts Registry

FreshStartsRegistry.com

Please note: This book is not intended to provide legal advice or replace professional legal counsel. It is a supportive, informational guide designed to help you feel more organized, empowered, and prepared as you navigate your divorce journey. Every situation is unique, and while this workbook offers tools, checklists, and general guidance, it is not a substitute for advice from a licensed attorney or financial professional. Use this book as a companion to your process—not as a legal directive—and always consult the appropriate experts for decisions specific to your case.

Contents

Divorce Lawyers 3

Divorce Coaches 22

Financial Planners 29

Mediators 33

Co-Parenting Coaches 39

Therapists 45

Real Estate Agents 51

Mortgage Lenders 55

Tax Advisors 63

Children's Therapists 67

Career Coaches 73

Self Help & Life Coaches 81

Professional Organizers 87

Fitness/Movement Coaches 93

Relationship Coaches 99

Additional Questions 105

Welcome, we're so glad you're here.

*We're really proud of you
for making a brave choice.*

Hey there,

Before we dive in, we want you to feel completely comfortable with this book. If the title feels too bold or you'd prefer a bit more privacy, just send us an email at hi@freshstartsregistry. com with your address, and we'll send you a discreet, no-fuss sticker to cover it up. Your comfort matters to us, always.

— The Fresh Starts Team

10 Things You Can Do to Prepare Yourself for the Divorce Process

Divorce can bring about emotional, financial, and practical challenges. Whether the decision to separate is mutual or one-sided, it's crucial to understand that preparing yourself to navigate the divorce process is of utmost importance. Taking the time to equip yourself with knowledge, support, and a clear plan can help you navigate this complex journey with greater confidence, resilience, and control over your future. We rounded up 10 reasons why preparation is key during divorce and how it can empower you to make informed decisions, protect your interests, and foster a smoother transition into the next chapter of your life.

1. **Gather financial documents:** Collect all relevant financial records, including bank statements, tax returns, investment statements, mortgage documents, and credit card statements. This information will help assess your financial situation, determine assets, debts, and income, and ensure a fair division during the divorce proceedings.

2. **Document expenses**: Keep track of your monthly expenses and create a budget. Understanding your financial needs and obligations will help you plan for post-divorce life and negotiate support payments effectively.

3. **Inventory assets and properties:** Make a comprehensive list of marital assets, such as real estate, vehicles, valuable items, and investments. It is crucial to have a clear understanding of what will need to be divided during the divorce process.

4. **Secure important documents:** Safeguard important legal documents, such as birth certificates, passports, marriage certificates, and insurance policies. Having access to these documents will make it easier to navigate legal processes and establish your identity and rights.

5. **Consider your children's needs:** If you have children, prioritize their well-being and consider their needs in terms of custody, visitation, and support. Understand the different types of custody arrangements and gather information about child support guidelines in your jurisdiction.

6. **Consult with professionals:** Seek advice from professionals such as divorce attorneys, financial advisors, and therapists. These experts can provide guidance, protect your rights, help you make informed decisions, and offer emotional support throughout the process.

7. **Educate yourself on divorce laws:** Research the divorce laws specific to your jurisdiction to gain an understanding of your rights, obligations, and the legal processes involved. Being informed will empower you during negotiations and discussions with your attorney.

8. **Explore dispute resolution options:** Familiarize yourself with alternative dispute resolution methods like mediation or collaborative divorce. These processes can offer a more amicable and cost-effective approach to resolving disputes, compared to litigation.

9. **Focus on self-care:** Divorce can be emotionally draining, so prioritize self-care. Seek support from friends, family, or a therapist, and engage in activities that promote your well-being. Taking care of yourself will help you navigate the process with a clearer mindset.

10. **Keep emotions in check:** Divorce can be emotionally charged, but it's important to maintain composure and approach discussions and negotiations with a level head. Emotions can cloud judgment and hinder effective decision-making. Taking a rational and pragmatic approach will lead to better outcomes. We highly recommend working with a divorce coach during this process. We have vetted divorce coaches in our Resource Guide, so remember to check them out!

Divorce Lawyers

What They Do: A divorce attorney provides legal representation, helping you understand your rights and advocating for your interests during negotiations or in court. They draft legal documents, negotiate settlements, and ensure your divorce is processed according to state law.

Why You Need Them: Divorce laws vary by state, and the legal process can be complex. An experienced attorney protects your financial interests, parental rights, and long-term well-being.

What to Say When You Reach Out: "Hi [Attorney's Name], I'm going through a divorce and am looking for legal guidance. I'd like to understand how you approach divorce cases, especially regarding [mention any specific issues like custody, asset division, or alimony]. Can we schedule a consultation?"

What They Can Help With:

- Filing divorce paperwork

- Representing you in court or mediation

- Negotiating property division and custody

- Drafting legal agreements

10 Essential Questions to Ask a Potential Divorce Lawyer

Divorce is a difficult and emotional process, and it is important to have an experienced and knowledgeable lawyer on your side. When interviewing potential divorce lawyers, there are a few key questions you should ask to ensure that you are getting the best possible representation. We've rounded up 10 of the top and best questions to ask a potential divorce attorney before signing any contracts and making any decisions!

1. **How long have you been practicing family law?** The length of time a lawyer has been practicing family law is an important factor to consider. You want to ensure that your lawyer has significant experience in handling divorce cases. Ask them how long they've been practicing family law, and what percentage of their cases are related to divorce. You should also ask about their success rate in handling divorce cases.

2. **What is your area of expertise?** Some lawyers specialize in certain areas of family law, such as child custody, divorce mediation, or collaborative law. If you have a specific issue that you need help with, it is important to find a lawyer who has experience in that area.

3. **Will you be the primary attorney on my case?** Some law firms have multiple attorneys, and it's essential to know who will be handling your case. Ask the lawyer if they will be the primary attorney on your case, or if someone else will be handling it. If someone else will be handling it, ask to meet with that attorney before signing a contract.

4. **What is your fee structure?** Lawyers typically charge by the hour or on a retainer basis. It is important to understand how much you will be charged before you hire a lawyer.Ask about their hourly rate, how they bill for their services, and what their retainer fee is. You should also ask about any additional fees that may arise during the divorce process.

5. **How will you communicate with me?** It is important to find a lawyer who is responsive to your calls and emails. You should also ask how often you can expect to meet with your lawyer.

6. **What is your availability?** It's crucial to know how available your lawyer will be during the divorce process. Ask about their availability and how they communicate with their clients. Do they respond promptly to emails and phone calls? Will they be available for in-person meetings if needed?

7. **What is your approach to divorce?** Some lawyers take a more aggressive approach to divorce, while others prefer to negotiate a settlement. It is important to find a lawyer who is willing to work with you to achieve your goals.

8. **Can you provide me with references?** Asking for references is a great way to get feedback from other clients about a lawyer's experience and representation.

9. **Do you feel comfortable representing me?** It is important to feel comfortable with your lawyer and to have confidence in their ability to represent you. If you do not feel comfortable with a lawyer, it is okay to find someone else.

10. **What is your experience with alternative dispute resolution options?** Ask about the lawyer's experience with alternative dispute resolution methods like mediation or collaborative divorce. Understanding their willingness to explore these options can be beneficial in achieving a more amicable resolution.

Find the Experts you need at freshstartsregistry.com/experts

It's important to remember that...

Divorce is a difficult process, but it is important to remember that you are not alone. With the help of an experienced and knowledgeable lawyer, you can get through this difficult time and come out stronger on the other side. Don't forget to reach out to any of our divorce coaches to prepare for your meetings. We've got you!

_____

_____

_____

_____

_____

_____

_____

_____

_____

_____

10 Questions About Child Custody to Ask Your Divorce Lawyer

Divorce is a deeply personal and emotionally charged process, especially when children are involved. As parents, ensuring the well-being and best interests of your children is paramount, making it crucial to have a clear understanding of child custody matters during a divorce. Your divorce lawyer becomes a critical ally in navigating this complex terrain, advocating for your rights and guiding you through the legal aspects of child custody. We rounded up 10 important questions about custody to ask your divorce lawyer, and explore the significance of asking these questions, as well as the reasons why doing so is essential in safeguarding your children's future and ensuring a fair and amicable parenting arrangement. By gaining clarity and arming yourself with knowledge, you can approach child custody negotiations with confidence and make informed decisions that prioritize your children's happiness and well-being.

1. **What are the different types of child custody arrangements, and what factors are considered in determining custody?**
   Understanding the types of custody, such as physical custody, legal custody, and joint custody, helps you grasp the available options and the factors that courts consider when making custody decisions. Here are 10 general questions to ask your divorce lawyer about child custody.

2. **What are the criteria for determining the best interests of the child?** Inquiring about the factors that courts consider in determining the best interests of the child helps you understand what aspects of your situation may influence custody decisions and how to present your case effectively.

3. **How is parenting time or visitation typically structured?** Understanding how parenting time or visitation schedules are usually established helps you anticipate the potential arrangement and develop a parenting plan that works for both you and your child.

4. **What are the potential implications of relocation or moving with a child after divorce?** If you anticipate needing to relocate after the divorce, understanding the legal implications, requirements, and potential impact on custody arrangements is crucial for making informed decisions.

5. **How can I demonstrate my ability to provide a stable and nurturing environment for my child?** Asking this question allows you to gather insights on how to present evidence and showcase your ability to provide a stable and supportive home environment, which can positively influence custody decisions.

6. **What are some common issues or disputes that arise regarding child custody, and how can they be resolved?** Learning about common challenges related to child custody and potential resolution methods helps you prepare for possible conflicts and explore effective solutions.

7. **How is child support determined, and what expenses does it cover?** Inquiring about child support helps you understand the financial obligations associated with caring for your child and ensures you have a clear understanding of the factors considered in calculating child support payments.

8. **How can co-parenting challenges be addressed and managed effectively?** Understanding strategies for effective co-parenting and addressing potential challenges helps promote a positive co-parenting relationship, which is beneficial for your child's well-being.

9. **Can custody arrangements be modified or adjusted in the future?** Inquiring about the possibility of modifying custody arrangements in the future is important as circumstances may change over time. Understanding the process for seeking modifications provides clarity for the long term.

10. **What resources or professionals can assist with child custody evaluations or assessments if needed?** In some cases, child custody evaluations may be necessary. Asking about resources and professionals who can assist with evaluations helps you understand the potential steps involved and the professionals' qualifications.

Asking these questions provides valuable information about child custody laws, considerations, and strategies, allowing you to be better prepared and make informed decisions throughout the divorce process. Remember that specific laws and practices may vary by jurisdiction, so consulting with your divorce lawyer is essential for personalized advice.

_____

_____

_____

_____

10 Questions About Alimony to Ask Your Divorce Lawyer

When going through a divorce, one of the most crucial aspects to address is alimony, also known as spousal support. Alimony can significantly impact your financial well-being post-divorce, making it essential to have a clear understanding of how it works and what to expect. To ensure you make informed decisions about alimony, it's crucial to ask your divorce lawyer pertinent questions. By actively engaging in the process and seeking clarifications, you can protect your interests and secure a fair outcome. We've rounded up 10 vital questions to ask your divorce lawyer about alimony and why these are key questions to have answered on your divorce journey.

What is alimony?

Alimony, in terms of a divorce, is money that one spouse pays to the other after they separate or get divorced. It is a way to support the spouse who may have a harder time financially after the marriage ends. The money is meant to help the person who earns less or doesn't have a job to cover their living expenses and maintain a similar lifestyle as they had during the marriage. Alimony is decided by a court or through an agreement between the spouses, and it can be temporary or last for a longer period of time.

1. **How is alimony determined, and what factors are considered in awarding alimony?** Understanding the factors that courts consider when determining alimony helps you grasp how your specific circumstances may influence the potential award.

2. **What are the different types of alimony or spousal support arrangements?** Inquiring about the various types of alimony, such as temporary, rehabilitative, or permanent, allows you to understand the available options and their implications.

3. **What is the duration of alimony payments, and how is it typically calculated?** Understanding how the duration and calculation of alimony payments are determined provides clarity on the length of financial support you may expect or be required to provide.

4. **Can alimony be modified or terminated in the future?** Asking about the possibility of modifying or terminating alimony helps you understand the circumstances under which alimony arrangements can be changed in the future.

5. **How does the length of the marriage impact alimony considerations?** Inquiring about the role of the duration of the marriage in alimony decisions helps you understand how the length of the marriage may affect the potential award or obligation.

6. **What financial factors and assets are considered in determining alimony?** Understanding the financial factors and assets that are taken into account when calculating alimony helps you assess the potential financial implications of the divorce.

7. **Are there tax implications associated with alimony payments?** Inquiring about the tax consequences of alimony payments helps you understand how alimony may impact your tax obligations and financial planning.

8. **How can I present evidence to support my case for or against alimony?** Understanding how to present evidence and build a strong case for or against alimony allows you to effectively advocate for your position during negotiations or court proceedings.

9. **Are there alternatives to alimony, such as lump-sum payments or property division, that may be considered?** Inquiring about alternatives to traditional alimony arrangements helps you explore different options that may better suit your circumstances or preferences.

10. **What steps can I take to protect my financial interests regarding alimony during the divorce process?** Asking this question allows you to gather insights on how to safeguard your financial interests, ensuring that alimony arrangements are fair and sustainable.

Asking these questions helps you gain a comprehensive understanding of alimony laws, considerations, and potential outcomes, allowing you to make informed decisions and protect your financial well-being throughout the divorce process. Remember to consult with a divorce lawyer to obtain personalized advice based on your specific situation and jurisdiction.

_____

_____

_____

_____

_____

10 Questions to Ask Your Divorce Lawyer About Your Home and Real Estate

Divorce is a challenging and emotionally charged process, and one aspect that often requires careful consideration is the division of real estate and the family home. Many individuals going through a divorce may overlook the importance of discussing real estate matters with their divorce lawyer. However, understanding the implications and asking pertinent questions about real estate during divorce can be crucial for protecting your interests and making informed decisions. We rounded up 10 questions about your real estate to ask your divorce lawyer and the key questions you should ask your attorney to ensure a smoother transition during this challenging time.

1. **How will our jointly owned property be divided during the divorce?** Inquiring about the division of jointly owned real estate helps you understand the potential outcomes and ensure a fair distribution of property.

2. **What factors are considered when determining the division of real estate in a divorce?** Understanding the factors that courts consider, such as the property's value, mortgage obligations, and contributions of each spouse, helps you grasp how these factors may influence the division.

3. **What are my options if I want to keep the marital home?** Asking about your options for retaining the marital home allows you to explore the possibility of negotiating a buyout, refinancing the mortgage, or considering other arrangements that align with your preferences and financial circumstances.

4. **How can we handle shared debts or mortgages associated with the property?** Inquiring about shared debts or mortgages helps you understand how these obligations will be addressed and whether one spouse will assume responsibility or if the property needs to be sold to satisfy the debts.

5. **Can I sell the property before the divorce is finalized?** Understanding whether you have the ability to sell the property during the divorce process helps you determine if it's a viable option and what considerations need to be taken into account.

6. **What happens if the real estate has appreciated in value during the marriage?** Asking about the treatment of any appreciation in value helps you understand if the increase in value will be considered as part of the marital assets and how it may impact the division of property.

7. **Can we agree to a co-ownership or shared arrangement for the real estate after the divorce?** Inquiring about the possibility of a co-ownership or shared arrangement post-divorce allows you to explore alternative solutions that may be suitable for both parties and the property in question.

8. **What potential tax implications should I be aware of regarding the real estate in the divorce?** Understanding the tax consequences associated with the real estate, such as capital gains tax or tax deductions, helps you make informed decisions and plan your financial affairs effectively.

9. **Are there any legal restrictions or considerations regarding the sale or transfer of the real estate during the divorce process?** Inquiring about any legal restrictions or considerations helps ensure that you adhere to the necessary legal requirements and avoid potential complications when dealing with real estate in the divorce.

10. **How can I protect my interests in real estate during the divorce process?** Asking this question allows you to gather insights on how to safeguard your rights, ensure a fair division, and protect your financial interests related to the real estate involved in the divorce.

_____

_____

Asking these questions provides valuable information about the division, options, and considerations related to real estate in divorce proceedings. It's essential to consult with a divorce lawyer to obtain personalized advice based on your specific situation and jurisdiction.

_____

_____

_____

_____

_____

_____

_____

10 Questions About Dividing Up Your Property and Assets for a Divorce Lawyer

Divorce is a life-altering event that brings about significant changes, particularly in the division of property and assets. Amid the emotional turmoil, it is crucial to engage in open and thorough communication with your divorce lawyer about dividing your property and discussing your assets. Many individuals underestimate the importance of these discussions and fail to ask pertinent questions about the division process. However, understanding the intricacies involved and seeking guidance from your attorney can have a profound impact on safeguarding your financial future. We rounded up 10 questions to ask your divorce lawyer about dividing up your assets and property, shedding light on potential complexities, highlighting the significance of fair distribution, and providing key questions to ask your attorney to ensure a smooth transition into your post-divorce life.

1. **How is property divided during a divorce, and what factors are considered?** Understanding the process and factors considered by the courts, such as the length of the marriage, financial contributions, and individual needs, helps you grasp the potential outcomes and ensure a fair division.

2. **What is considered marital property and separate property?** Inquiring about the distinction between marital property (acquired during the marriage) and separate property (owned prior to marriage or acquired through inheritance/gift) helps determine what assets are subject to division.

3. **How can we identify and value our assets for division?** Asking about the process of identifying and valuing assets ensures a comprehensive assessment, including real estate, investments, retirement accounts, vehicles, and personal belongings, to facilitate an equitable division.

4. **Can we negotiate a property settlement agreement outside of court?** Inquiring about the possibility of negotiating a settlement agreement helps explore alternatives to a court-ordered division, allowing you and your spouse to have more control over the outcome.

5. **What options are available if we have complex or high-value assets?** Asking about options for handling complex assets, such as businesses, stock options, or intellectual property, ensures you address their unique considerations and seek expert guidance when necessary.

6. **How are debts divided in a divorce?** Understanding how debts, such as mortgages, loans, or credit card debts, are handled during the division process helps you grasp the potential responsibility and implications associated with each debt.

7. **Can we agree to an unequal division of property, and how is that handled legally?** Inquiring about the possibility of an unequal division allows you to explore options based on specific circumstances, such as one spouse's financial needs or contributions, while understanding the legal considerations involved.

8. **What role does documentation and evidence play in property division?** Asking about the importance of documentation, such as financial records, property titles, or prenuptial agreements, helps you understand the significance of supporting evidence in establishing ownership and value.

9. **Can property division be modified or revisited after the divorce is finalized?** Inquiring about the potential for modifying property division arrangements helps you understand if there are circumstances that may warrant a reassessment in the future.

10. **How can I protect my interests in the division of property during the divorce process?** Asking this question allows you to gather insights on how to safeguard your rights, ensure a fair division, and protect your financial interests related to the property involved in the divorce.

Asking these questions provides valuable information about the division of property in a divorce, enabling you to make informed decisions and protect your financial well-being. Keep in mind that divorce laws and processes may vary by jurisdiction, so it's important to consult with a divorce lawyer for personalized advice based on your specific situation.

_____

_____

_____

_____

_____

_____

_____

10 Questions About Custody of Your Family Pets and Animals for a Divorce Lawyer

Divorce is a complex and emotionally charged process, and amidst the legalities and negotiations, it is often the welfare of our beloved pets and animals that gets overlooked. As cherished members of our families, our furry companions deserve special consideration when it comes to custody arrangements. That's why consulting a divorce lawyer specifically trained in pet custody matters is a crucial step to ensure the well-being and happiness of our four-legged friends during this challenging time. We rounded up 10 questions to ask a divorce lawyer about the custody arrangement of your family pets, and the reasons why it is essential to have open conversations with a divorce lawyer about the custody arrangement for your family pet or animals. By seeking expert legal guidance, we can protect the best interests of our beloved pets and find mutually beneficial solutions that prioritize their happiness and continued bond with both parties involved.

1. **How is custody of animals typically determined in divorce cases?** This question is important to gain a general understanding of the process and potential outcomes regarding pet custody.

2. **What factors do the courts consider when deciding custody of pets?** Understanding the criteria used by the courts helps you prepare a strong case for why you should be granted custody of your animals.

3. **Can we include a specific pet custody arrangement in our divorce agreement?** Asking about the possibility of a customized pet custody arrangement allows you to explore options that align with your preferences and the well-being of your animals.

4. **Are there any laws or regulations in our jurisdiction that specifically address pet custody?** Knowing if there are any specific laws or regulations pertaining to pet custody in your jurisdiction helps you navigate the legal process more effectively.

5. **What evidence or documentation should I gather to support my case for pet custody?** Asking this question helps you understand what kind of evidence or documentation you should gather, such as records of pet care, expenses, or your bond with the animals, to strengthen your case for custody.

6. **Can we seek joint custody or visitation rights for our pets?** Inquiring about joint custody or visitation rights demonstrates your commitment to maintaining a meaningful relationship with your animals and ensures you explore all available options.

7. **How will decisions about pet care and expenses be addressed in the divorce agreement?** It is important to clarify how decisions regarding pet care, such as veterinary expenses, training, or long-term care, will be addressed to ensure the well-being of your animals is adequately provided for.

8. **What happens if we cannot agree on custody of our pets?** Understanding the potential consequences or alternatives if an agreement cannot be reached can help you prepare for various scenarios and explore alternative dispute resolution methods, such as mediation or negotiation.

9. **Can the court consider the best interests of the animals when determining custody?** Asking this question highlights your concern for the welfare of your pets and ensures that their best interests are taken into account during the decision-making process.

10. Are there any precedents or past cases related to pet custody that could influence our case? Inquiring about past cases or precedents helps you understand how similar situations have been resolved in the past, providing insights into potential outcomes and strategies for presenting your case effectively.

_____

_____

_____

_____

_____

_____

_____

_____

_____

_____

Divorce Coaches

What They Do: A divorce coach helps you manage the emotional and practical aspects of divorce. They support goal-setting, decision-making, and emotional resilience, while also guiding you through the transition.

Why You Need Them: Divorce can feel overwhelming, and it's easy to lose focus. A coach keeps you grounded and helps you make informed, thoughtful decisions.

What to Say When You Reach Out: "Hi [Coach's Name], I'm in the process of a divorce and feeling overwhelmed. I'm looking for support to navigate the emotional and practical challenges. Can you tell me more about your approach?"

What They Can Help With:

- Emotional regulation

- Setting realistic goals

- Coping strategies

- Creating a post-divorce plan

10 Reasons to Work with a Divorce Coach During Your Divorce Process

Divorce is a challenging and emotionally charged process that can leave individuals feeling overwhelmed and uncertain about the future. During this difficult time, working with a divorce coach can provide invaluable support and guidance. A divorce coach is a trained professional who specializes in helping individuals navigate the complexities of divorce. Keep on reading to explore why it is beneficial to work with a divorce coach and shed light on what a divorce coach is. By understanding the role of a divorce coach and the advantages they offer, you can make an informed decision about seeking their assistance to navigate your divorce more effectively.

1. Emotional support: Divorce often triggers intense emotions, such as anger, grief, or fear. A divorce coach can provide a safe and supportive environment for you to express these emotions and work through them constructively. They offer empathy, understanding, and techniques to help you cope with the emotional challenges of divorce, empowering you to make sound decisions based on clarity rather than heightened emotions.

2. Clarity and guidance: A divorce coach helps you gain clarity about your goals, priorities, and values, enabling you to make well-informed decisions during the divorce process. Navigating the legal, financial, and practical aspects of divorce can be overwhelming. A divorce coach can help you develop a strategic plan tailored to your unique circumstances. They can assist in organizing your thoughts, gathering necessary information, and understanding the implications of various choices. With their expertise, you can approach negotiations, settlements, and court proceedings more confidently, ensuring your interests are protected.

3. Personal empowerment: Working with a divorce coach helps you develop self-confidence and regain a sense of control over your life during this challenging time.

4. Communication skills: A divorce coach can help you improve your communication skills, facilitating more effective conversations and negotiations with your spouse and other involved parties. Effective communication is vital during divorce, especially when dealing with a co-parent or negotiating with your ex-spouse. A divorce coach can provide guidance on how to express yourself clearly, assertively, and constructively. They can help you navigate difficult conversations, manage conflict, and maintain respectful communication throughout the process. Improved communication skills can lead to more positive outcomes and minimize unnecessary stress and hostility.

5. Co-parenting guidance: If you have children, a divorce coach can provide valuable guidance on co-parenting strategies, helping you establish a healthy and cooperative parenting dynamic with your ex-spouse.

6. Conflict resolution: A divorce coach can help you navigate conflict and provide techniques for managing disagreements in a constructive and respectful manner.

7. Decision-making support: With their guidance, a divorce coach can assist you in making important decisions regarding property division, child custody, and other aspects of the divorce process. A divorce coach can help you clarify your goals and priorities for the divorce process and beyond. They assist in identifying what matters most to you and support you in making decisions aligned with your values and long-term objectives. By working with a divorce coach, you can gain a clearer perspective on your desired outcomes and feel more empowered to navigate the complexities of divorce with purpose.

8. Resource and referral network: A divorce coach often has a network of professionals, such as lawyers, therapists, and financial advisors, whom they can refer you to for additional support and guidance.

9. Financial awareness: A divorce coach can help you understand the financial aspects of the divorce process, empowering you to make informed decisions regarding assets, debts, and financial settlements.

10. Post-divorce transition support: A divorce coach can provide guidance and support as you navigate the post-divorce transition, helping you rebuild your life and move forward with confidence.

_____

_____

_____

_____

_____

10 Essential Questions to Ask a Potential Divorce Coach

Divorce is a monumental life transition, and navigating its complexities often requires more than just legal support. A divorce coach can provide the emotional guidance, practical planning, and strategic thinking needed to move through this time with clarity and confidence. Whether you're considering divorce, actively in the process, or rebuilding after separation, finding the right coach can make all the difference. Here are ten essential questions to ask when selecting a divorce coach to ensure you find the perfect fit for your journey.

1. **What is your experience with divorce coaching?** Not all coaches are created equal. Ask about their specific experience with divorce coaching, including how many clients they've helped, their understanding of divorce law (if applicable), and their background in handling the emotional and practical challenges of divorce.

2. **What type of support do you offer?** Divorce coaching can encompass a variety of support types, including emotional resilience, decision-making strategies, co-parenting plans, and financial clarity. Make sure the coach you choose specializes in the areas where you need the most guidance.

3. **How do you help clients navigate high-conflict situations?** If your divorce involves high-conflict dynamics, you'll want a coach who is well-versed in de-escalation strategies and conflict resolution. Ask how they handle situations involving narcissistic ex-partners, custody disputes, or legal challenges.

4. **Are you familiar with collaborative divorce and mediation?** A growing number of divorcing couples are choosing collaborative divorce or mediation over litigation. If this is a path you're considering, make sure your coach understands the process and can guide you effectively.

5. **What strategies do you use for emotional healing and resilience?** Divorce isn't just a legal event; it's an emotional one too. Ask your coach about the tools and strategies they use to help clients build emotional resilience, manage stress, and heal from the loss.

6. **How do you support clients with co-parenting plans?** If you have children, co-parenting will be a significant part of your life post-divorce. Ask your coach if they can help you create effective co-parenting strategies and communication plans to minimize conflict and prioritize your children's well-being.

7. **What is your availability and preferred method of communication?** Understanding your coach's availability is crucial. Ask if they offer virtual sessions, in-person meetings, or text and email support for quick questions and urgent needs.

8. **How do you measure progress and success?** Divorce coaching should be goal-oriented and results-driven. Inquire about how your coach measures progress, sets milestones, and evaluates success throughout the coaching process.

9. **Do you work alongside other professionals like lawyers or financial planners?** A well-connected divorce coach can be invaluable, particularly if they collaborate with attorneys, financial advisors, and mediators. This holistic approach ensures you have a full spectrum of support.

10. **What can I expect from our coaching sessions?** Understanding the structure of your sessions can help set expectations. Ask about the length of each session, the frequency of meetings, and what typical sessions include—like goal-setting, emotional check-ins, or strategic planning.

It's important to remember that…

Choosing the right divorce coach is a critical step toward reclaiming your confidence and building a life that aligns with your vision for the future. By asking these ten essential questions, you ensure that your coach is prepared, experienced, and capable of guiding you through the complexities of divorce with empathy and strategic insight.

_____

_____

_____

_____

_____

_____

_____

_____

_____

Financial Planners
Certified Divorce Financial Analysts (CDFA)

What They Do: A Certified Divorce Financial Analyst (CDFA) helps you understand the financial implications of divorce, including asset division, budgeting, and future planning.

Why You Need Them: Divorce often changes your financial landscape. A CDFA ensures that you make informed decisions that protect your financial future.

What to Say When You Reach Out: "Hi [Financial Planner's Name], I'm preparing for a divorce and need help understanding my financial situation. Can you help me plan for asset division and financial stability after the divorce?"

What They Can Help With:

- Analyzing financial documents
- Budgeting for post-divorce life
- Calculating alimony or child support
- Planning for retirement and investments

10 Questions to Ask Your Financial Advisor

Divorce is an emotionally and financially tumultuous time in one's life, often requiring careful consideration and strategic planning to protect your financial well-being. Amid the myriad of decisions you must make, consulting with a financial advisor may not be at the top of your list. However, discussing your divorce and assets with a trusted financial advisor is of utmost importance. Their expertise can provide invaluable guidance and help you navigate the complexities of dividing assets, ensuring a secure future. By taking proactive steps and seeking professional advice, you can empower yourself to make informed financial decisions and secure your financial future in the midst of divorce. Here are the 10 questions to ask your financial advisor about going through your divorce and what you need to know.

1. **What financial steps should I take to prepare for the divorce process?** Asking this question helps you understand the initial actions you should take to protect your financial interests during the divorce.

2. **How can I establish a post-divorce budget and financial plan?** Inquiring about creating a budget and financial plan after the divorce helps you gain clarity on your financial situation and set realistic goals for the future.

3. **What are the potential tax implications of the divorce settlement?** Understanding the tax consequences of the settlement helps you plan for any tax obligations and optimize your financial outcomes.

4. **How can I protect my assets and investments during the divorce?** Asking about strategies to safeguard your assets and investments during the divorce process helps you ensure their proper treatment and minimize the risk of financial losses.

5. **What considerations should I keep in mind regarding property division?** Inquiring about the financial aspects of property division helps you understand the potential implications and make informed decisions about which assets to pursue or relinquish.

6. **Can you help me evaluate the long-term financial impact of different settlement options?** Asking for assistance in evaluating the financial implications of different settlement scenarios helps you make informed decisions about which options align best with your financial goals.

7. **How can I handle joint debts and liabilities effectively?** Inquiring about strategies for addressing joint debts and liabilities helps you understand your options and responsibilities, ensuring a fair distribution of financial obligations.

8. **What changes should I make to my investment and retirement accounts in light of the divorce?** Asking for guidance on adjusting your investment and retirement accounts helps you align your financial strategies with your post-divorce goals and aspirations.

9. **Can you assist me in understanding and evaluating the financial aspects of child support and alimony?** Inquiring about the financial implications of child support and alimony payments helps you understand the potential impact on your financial situation and plan accordingly.

10. **What other professionals, such as tax experts or estate planners, should I consider consulting during the divorce process?** Asking for recommendations on other professionals to involve in your divorce, such as tax experts or estate planners, helps ensure that you have a comprehensive support network to address various financial aspects.

By asking these questions, you can gain valuable insights from your financial advisor about how to navigate the financial complexities of divorce. Remember to consult with a qualified professional who specializes in divorce-related financial matters to obtain personalized advice based on your specific situation.

_____

_____

_____

_____

_____

_____

_____

_____

_____

_____

Mediators

What They Do: A mediator facilitates communication between divorcing parties to reach a mutually agreeable settlement without going to court.

Why You Need Them: Mediation is typically faster and less costly than litigation. It's useful when both parties are willing to negotiate.

What to Say When You Reach Out: "Hi [Mediator's Name], I'm looking to pursue mediation for my divorce. Can you explain how your process works and what to expect during sessions?"

What They Can Help With:

- Facilitating negotiation

- Drafting settlement agreements

- Addressing custody and financial arrangements

- Reducing conflict and fostering cooperation

10 Essential Questions to Ask a Potential Divorce Mediator

Divorce is challenging, but mediation can make the process more manageable, less adversarial, and often more cost-effective than litigation. A skilled mediator acts as a neutral party to help you and your spouse reach agreements on critical issues like property division, child custody, and financial support. However, not all mediators are the same, and finding the right fit is crucial. Here are 10 essential questions to ask a potential divorce mediator to ensure they're the right choice for your situation.

---

1. **What is your experience with divorce mediation?** Divorce mediation requires a deep understanding of family law, conflict resolution, and the emotional intricacies of divorce. A mediator with extensive experience will be better equipped to handle complex issues and navigate conflicts smoothly.

   Follow-Up Questions:

   - How many divorce mediations have you handled?
   - Are you familiar with high-conflict divorces?
   - Have you mediated cases with child custody disputes or complex asset division?

2. **Are you a certified mediator?** Certification ensures that the mediator has completed formal training and adheres to professional standards. Different states have varying requirements, so it's crucial to confirm their credentials.

   Follow-Up Questions:

   - What certifications do you hold?
   - Are you affiliated with any professional mediation organizations?
   - Do you participate in continuing education?

3. **What is your mediation style? (Facilitative, evaluative, or transformative)** mediators typically use one of three styles:

   - Facilitative: Focuses on guiding both parties to mutual agreement without offering personal opinions.
   - Evaluative: More directive, sometimes offering opinions on legal matters.
   - Transformative: Focuses on empowering the parties to resolve their own conflicts.

Understanding their approach helps you determine if it matches your needs and communication style.

   Follow-Up Questions:

   - How do you handle high-conflict discussions?
   - Do you offer guidance or only facilitate dialogue?

Find the Experts you need at freshstartsregistry.com/experts

4. **How do you handle impasses during mediation?** Mediation sometimes hits a roadblock where neither party can agree. Knowing how a mediator handles these situations is crucial for keeping the process moving forward.

   Follow-Up Questions:

   - Do you bring in additional experts if needed?
   - What techniques do you use to break through deadlocks?

5. **Do you mediate all issues, including child custody and financial agreements?** Some mediators only handle financial matters or property division, while others are equipped to address sensitive topics like child custody and support. Ensure they are capable of handling all aspects of your divorce.

   Follow-Up Questions:

   - Are you comfortable mediating high-conflict custody disputes?
   - How do you address child support and spousal support negotiations?

6. **How long does the mediation process typically take?** Understanding the timeline helps you set expectations. A well-organized mediator can often complete the process in weeks or months, depending on the complexity of the case.

   Follow-Up Questions:

   - What is the average number of sessions required?
   - Do you set timelines for agreement on specific issues?

7. **What are your fees, and how are they structured?** Mediation is typically more cost-effective than litigation, but fees can still vary widely. Understanding the cost structure upfront helps prevent surprises.

Follow-Up Questions:

- Do you charge per session or a flat fee?
- Are there additional costs for document preparation or filing?
- What is your cancellation policy?

8. **Do you draft the final divorce agreement?** Some mediators draft the final agreement, while others only provide a memorandum of understanding that you must take to a lawyer. Knowing this upfront clarifies the next steps after mediation concludes.

Follow-Up Questions:

- Is your draft legally binding, or does it require review by an attorney?
- Do you file the documents with the court?

9. **How do you ensure confidentiality during mediation?** Mediation is confidential, but understanding the specific measures taken to protect your privacy is important, especially if sensitive financial or custody issues are discussed.

Follow-Up Questions:

- Do you keep written records of our sessions?
- What steps do you take to protect my personal information?
- Are the discussions admissible in court if mediation fails?

10. How do you handle communication with both parties?
Transparency and balanced communication are key in mediation. A good mediator remains neutral, ensures both voices are heard, and facilitates productive dialogue.

Follow-Up Questions:

- Do you communicate separately with each party if needed?
- How do you manage power imbalances in conversations?
- Are there follow-up sessions after agreements are made?

_____

It's important to remember that...

Selecting the right mediator can be the difference between a smooth, collaborative divorce process and one fraught with conflict. By asking these ten essential questions, you equip yourself with the knowledge to make an informed decision. Remember, the right mediator isn't just experienced—they are a skilled communicator, neutral facilitator, and a strong advocate for resolution and fairness.

_____

_____

_____

_____

_____

Co-Parenting Coaches

What They Do: A co-parenting coach helps divorced or separated parents develop effective communication and parenting plans that focus on the child's well-being.

Why You Need Them: Successful co-parenting requires clear communication and conflict management. A coach helps set boundaries and establish routines.

What to Say When You Reach Out: "Hi [Coach's Name], I'm navigating co-parenting after my divorce and need help creating a structured plan that minimizes conflict. Can you guide me through this process?"

What They Can Help With:

- Creating co-parenting agreements

- Improving communication with your ex

- Setting boundaries and parenting routines

- Managing conflicts related to parenting decisions

10 Essential Questions to Ask a Potential Co-Parenting Coach

Navigating co-parenting during or after a divorce can be incredibly challenging. A co-parenting coach helps bridge the communication gap, mediate conflicts, and provide strategies to create a healthy environment for your children. Finding the right co-parenting coach means asking the right questions to understand their approach, expertise, and compatibility with your family's needs. Here are 10 essential questions to ask a potential co-parenting coach to ensure they are the right fit for your family dynamics.

1. **What is Your Experience with Co-Parenting and High-Conflict Situations?** Co-parenting is already complex, but if your divorce is high-conflict, you need someone experienced in managing tension and mediating disputes. An experienced coach will have proven strategies to handle stubborn disagreements and help create a peaceful environment for your children.**Follow-Up Questions:**

   ◦ How many families have you worked with?
   ◦ Do you specialize in high-conflict co-parenting?
   ◦ Have you worked with families with special needs children or complex custody arrangements?

2. What is Your Coaching Philosophy and Approach? Different coaches have different philosophies. Some are solution-focused, while others are more emotionally driven. It's important to understand whether their approach matches your communication style and family needs.

Follow-Up Questions:

- Are your methods more directive or collaborative?
- Do you use structured plans or is it more fluid based on needs?
- How do you handle situations where one parent is uncooperative?

3. How do you support effective communication between co-parents? One of the biggest challenges in co-parenting is communication. A good coach provides tools and strategies for clear, conflict-free discussions about your children.

Follow-Up Questions:

- Do you use communication apps or structured meeting agendas?
- How do you handle misunderstandings or disagreements?
- What strategies do you teach for non-confrontational communication?

4. Do you provide guidance on parenting plans and custody arrangements? A well-structured parenting plan is the backbone of successful co-parenting. Your coach should be able to help you design a schedule that is fair, realistic, and child-focused.

Follow-Up Questions:

- Do you help create customized parenting plans?
- Can you assist with modifications if circumstances change?
- Are you familiar with state custody laws?

5. **How do you handle co-parenting conflicts?** Conflict is often unavoidable, but how it's managed makes all the difference. A co-parenting coach should have proven methods to de-escalate tension and keep discussions focused on solutions.

   Follow-Up Questions:

   - What are your go-to conflict resolution strategies?
   - How do you mediate when one parent is uncooperative?
   - Do you involve children in conflict resolution?

6. **Do you work with blended families or extended family dynamics?** If you or your ex-spouse have remarried or have new partners, the dynamics of co-parenting change. A coach experienced with blended families can help you navigate boundaries, roles, and expectations.

   Follow-Up Questions:

   - Do you provide guidance for step-parent relationships?
   - How do you manage grandparent involvement or other extended family members?
   - What strategies do you recommend for integrating new partners?

7. **How do you measure progress in co-parenting?** Tracking progress is crucial to understand if the coaching is effective. Your coach should have clear methods for evaluating improvements in communication, conflict resolution, and overall harmony.

   Follow-Up Questions:

   - Do you set measurable goals during sessions?
   - How do you track improvements in communication and conflict management?
   - Do you adjust your approach based on progress?

8. **Are sessions in-person, virtual, or both?** Flexibility in meeting formats can make co-parenting coaching more accessible and consistent, especially if parents live far apart or have demanding schedules.

   Follow-Up Questions:

   - Do you offer virtual sessions?
   - Are there options for evening or weekend appointments?
   - Can both parents join remotely if needed?

9. **What are your fees, and how are they structured?** Understanding costs upfront helps prevent surprises. Some coaches charge hourly rates, while others offer packages. Make sure their rates fit within your budget and expectations.

   Follow-Up Questions:

   - Do you charge per session or offer packages?
   - Are there additional costs for written parenting plans or follow-up support?
   - What is your cancellation policy?

10. **Can you provide references or testimonials?** Testimonials and references provide insight into a coach's effectiveness and communication style. Hearing from past clients can help you gauge if they're the right fit for your family.

    Follow-Up Questions:

    - Can you share testimonials from past clients?
    - Are you willing to provide references?
    - Do you have success stories of high-conflict co-parenting situations?

It's important to remember that…

Finding the right co-parenting coach is a crucial step in ensuring stability and harmony for your children post-divorce. By asking these ten essential questions, you gain clarity on the coach's experience, style, and methods for managing conflict and improving communication. A skilled co-parenting coach can turn a difficult situation into a more peaceful, child-focused partnership that benefits everyone involved.

_____

_____

_____

_____

_____

_____

_____

_____

_____

Therapists

What They Do: A therapist helps you work through the emotional and psychological challenges of divorce.

Why You Need Them: Divorce can trigger grief, anxiety, and identity struggles. A therapist helps you process emotions and regain confidence.

What to Say When You Reach Out: "Hi, I'm going through a divorce and need support processing the emotional challenges. Do you specialize in divorce recovery and family transitions?"

What They Can Help With:

- Grief and loss

- Managing stress and anxiety

- Building self-esteem post-divorce

- Navigating relationship changes

- Supporting children emotionally

10 Reasons to Work with a Therapist During Your Divorce Process

Divorce is a significant life event that can bring about a wide range of emotions and challenges. During this trying time, seeking support from a therapist can be incredibly beneficial. A therapist is a trained mental health professional who can provide guidance, emotional support, and valuable coping strategies to help individuals navigate the complexities of divorce. We've rounded up 10 reasons to work with a therapist during your divorce and why working with a therapist during a divorce is essential. By understanding the valuable role a therapist plays in promoting emotional well-being and facilitating the healing process, you can make an informed decision to prioritize your mental health during this transitional period.

1. Emotional support: Going through a divorce can be emotionally challenging, and a therapist provides a safe and supportive space to express and process your feelings. Divorce can trigger a whirlwind of emotions, including sadness, anger, anxiety, and grief. A therapist can offer a safe and confidential space for you to express and process these emotions. They provide empathetic support and help you navigate the challenges of divorce while offering valuable coping strategies to manage stress, maintain self-care, and foster emotional resilience.

2. Coping with grief and loss: Divorce often involves grieving the loss of a significant relationship. A therapist can help you navigate the grief process and provide tools for coping and healing.

3. Managing stress and anxiety: Divorce can be a highly stressful and anxiety-inducing experience. A therapist can teach you coping mechanisms and stress reduction techniques to manage these emotions effectively. The divorce process can be overwhelming, with numerous decisions to make, legal procedures to navigate, and changes to adjust to. A therapist can equip you with effective stress management techniques and anxiety reduction strategies. They help you develop healthy coping mechanisms, mindfulness practices, and relaxation techniques that promote emotional well-being and empower you to face the challenges ahead.

4. Building resilience: Working with a therapist during a divorce can help you develop resilience, which is crucial for navigating the challenges and uncertainties that arise during the process. Divorce can take a toll on self-esteem and self-confidence. A therapist can guide you in prioritizing self-care practices that promote overall well-being and assist in rebuilding self-esteem. They can help you identify your strengths, set boundaries, and develop healthy habits that contribute to your emotional and physical health during this challenging time.

5. Improving communication skills: A therapist can help you improve your communication skills, enabling more effective and constructive interactions with your ex-spouse, children, and other individuals involved in the divorce.

6. Co-parenting guidance: If you have children, a therapist can provide guidance on developing a healthy co-parenting relationship, ensuring the well-being of your children and facilitating effective communication and collaboration with your ex-spouse. If children are involved, co-parenting and managing family dynamics can be particularly challenging during and after a divorce. A therapist can offer guidance and support in navigating co-parenting arrangements, facilitating effective communication, and managing potential conflicts. They can help you prioritize the best interests of your children and establish a healthy foundation for a new family dynamic.

Find the Experts you need at freshstartsregistry.com/experts

7. Identifying and setting boundaries: Divorce often requires establishing new boundaries and redefining relationships. A therapist can assist you in identifying and setting healthy boundaries for yourself and your relationships moving forward.

8. Self-reflection and personal growth: The divorce process can be an opportunity for self-reflection and personal growth. A therapist can guide you in exploring your needs, values, and goals, helping you discover a stronger sense of self.

9. Managing the impact on children: If you have children, a therapist can help you understand and mitigate the impact of divorce on their emotional well-being, providing guidance on how to support them through the process.

10. Creating a post-divorce life plan: A therapist can assist you in creating a post-divorce life plan, helping you set goals, identify resources, and develop strategies to rebuild and thrive in your new chapter.

_____

_____

_____

_____

_____

_____

10 Essential Questions to Ask a Potential Therapist

Navigating the complexities of divorce is a deeply personal and emotionally charged journey. Whether you're considering divorce, actively going through the process, or working to rebuild your life post-divorce, the right therapist can be a lifeline of support and guidance. However, finding the right fit is crucial. Here are ten essential questions to ask when choosing a therapist for divorce-related support, ensuring you find someone who truly understands your journey.

1. **What is your experience with divorce counseling?** Divorce is a unique life event, and not all therapists specialize in its emotional and practical complexities. Look for a therapist with specific experience in divorce counseling who understands the nuances of grief, co-parenting struggles, and rebuilding self-identity.

2. **Are you familiar with high-conflict divorces?** If you're navigating a high-conflict divorce involving legal battles or complex family dynamics, you need someone well-versed in managing high-stress and emotionally charged situations.

3. **Do you offer support for co-parenting challenges?** Post-divorce co-parenting comes with its own set of challenges. Ask if the therapist can provide strategies for communication, conflict resolution, and supporting children emotionally through the transition.

4. **What therapeutic methods do you use?** Different therapists employ different therapeutic styles—like cognitive behavioral therapy (CBT), narrative therapy, or family systems therapy. Understanding their approach can help you decide if it aligns with your needs and healing style.

5. **Are you comfortable discussing financial anxiety related to divorce?** Divorce often brings financial concerns that impact emotional well-being. A therapist comfortable discussing financial anxiety, budgeting, and money-related stressors can be incredibly beneficial.

6. **How do you help clients navigate post-divorce life?** Your journey doesn't end with the finalization of divorce papers. A good therapist will help you process grief, redefine your identity, and build a new life with confidence.

7. **Can you support me through legal and custody discussions?** While therapists aren't legal advisors, they can provide emotional support and coping strategies during legal discussions, custody battles, and court appearances.

8. **What strategies do you use for managing divorce-related stress and anxiety?** Divorce can bring waves of anxiety, fear, and stress. Understanding how a therapist manages these emotions can help you gauge their ability to support you effectively.

9. **Are sessions available online?** The option for virtual therapy sessions can be a game-changer, especially when juggling legal meetings, work obligations, and parenting responsibilities.

10. **Do you work with other professionals like mediators or financial advisors?** Collaborative therapy that includes communication with mediators, financial planners, or divorce coaches can provide a holistic approach to your healing process.

It's important to remember that...

Choosing the right therapist is a powerful step toward emotional healing and empowerment during your divorce journey. By asking these critical questions, you can ensure you're working with someone equipped to support you through the unique challenges of separation and the path forward.

Real Estate Agents

What They Do: A real estate agent specializing in divorce can help you sell your marital home or find new housing.

Why You Need Them: Managing property sales during divorce requires sensitivity and an understanding of equitable division.

What to Say When You Reach Out: "Hi, I'm going through a divorce and need to sell our family home. Do you have experience with divorce-related property sales?"

What They Can Help With:

- Home valuation and listing

- Coordinating with both parties

- Selling or refinancing marital property

- Finding new housing

- Managing emotional stress during property transitions

10 Essential Questions to Your Real Estate Agent

Divorce brings about numerous challenges, particularly when it comes to matters surrounding your home. Amid the emotional strain and complex legalities, it is easy to overlook the importance of engaging in open conversations with your realtor about your property. However, seeking guidance from a knowledgeable real estate professional during a divorce can prove to be invaluable. Their expertise can help you navigate through the intricacies of selling, retaining, or dividing your home, ensuring that you make informed decisions that align with your goals and financial well-being. We rounded up 10 questions to ask your realtor during a divorce, highlighting their role in guiding you through the real estate aspect of your separation, and providing essential questions to ask them. By leveraging their expertise, you can approach your home matters with confidence, ultimately finding the best solution for your changing circumstances.

1. **How can a realtor assist me in selling our marital home during the divorce?** Asking this question helps you understand the realtor's role in the selling process and how they can support you in achieving a successful sale.

2. **What is the current market value of our home?** Inquiring about the market value helps you establish a realistic price range and ensures that you have accurate information when making decisions regarding the property.

3. **How can we best prepare our home for sale?** Asking for advice on preparing your home for sale helps you understand what improvements or staging may be necessary to enhance its market appeal and potentially increase its value.

4. **What is the optimal timeline for selling our home?** Inquiring about the ideal timeframe for selling your home allows you to plan your transition and align it with other aspects of the divorce process.

5. **Can you provide information about recent comparable sales in our area?** Asking for recent comparable sales helps you gauge the market activity and determine a competitive listing price for your home.

6. **What marketing strategies will you employ to attract potential buyers?** Inquiring about the realtor's marketing strategies allows you to assess their approach in reaching a wide range of potential buyers and increasing the visibility of your property.

7. **How will you handle showings and negotiations with potential buyers?** Asking about the realtor's process for showings and negotiations helps you understand how they will represent your interests during these crucial stages of the home-selling process.

8. **Can you assist us in finding suitable alternative housing options?** Inquiring about the realtor's ability to help you find new housing options allows you to leverage their expertise and potentially simplify your transition.

9. **What fees or commissions should we expect when selling our home?** Asking about the realtor's fees and commissions helps you understand the financial implications of their services and ensures that you are prepared for these costs.

10. Are there any legal considerations we should be aware of regarding the sale of our home during the divorce process?
Inquiring about any legal considerations helps you ensure compliance with local laws and regulations, minimizing potential complications or delays in the sale.

_____

Asking these questions will help you gather important information and make informed decisions about selling your marital home during the divorce process. Remember to consult with a realtor who specializes in divorce-related real estate transactions for personalized advice based on your specific situation and location.

_____

_____

_____

_____

_____

_____

_____

_____

Mortgage Lenders or Brokers

What They Do: A mortgage lender helps you refinance the marital home or secure a new mortgage post-divorce.

Why You Need Them: You may need to buy out your spouse or purchase a new home, both of which can be financially complex.

What to Say When You Reach Out: "Hi, I'm going through a divorce and considering refinancing or buying a new home. Do you specialize in divorce-related mortgage solutions?"

What They Can Help With:

- Refinancing existing mortgages
- Securing loans as a single applicant
- Navigating credit changes after divorce
- Understanding mortgage affordability

10 Questions to Ask a Mortgage Lender When Refinancing Your House During a Divorce

Refinancing your house during a divorce can be a complex and emotionally charged process. To navigate this important financial decision successfully, it is crucial to ask the right questions. Making informed choices can help protect your interests and ensure a smoother transition as you move forward. In this article, we will explore the key questions you should ask when refinancing your house during a divorce and why it is essential to seek clarity on these matters. By understanding the importance of these questions, you can confidently make decisions that align with your needs and secure a stable financial future. Here are 10 questions to ask your mortgage lender when refinancing your house during a divorce.

1. **Is refinancing the house a viable option for me during the divorce?** Asking this question helps you assess whether refinancing is a feasible solution based on your financial circumstances and goals.

2. **What is the current interest rate and how does it compare to my existing mortgage?** Inquiring about the current interest rate allows you to evaluate whether refinancing can potentially secure a lower rate, which may result in lower monthly payments or long-term savings.

3. **What are the costs associated with refinancing the house?** Asking about the refinancing costs, such as closing costs, appraisal fees, and lender fees, helps you understand the financial implications of the refinancing process.

4. **Can I qualify for a mortgage on my own?** Inquiring about your eligibility for a mortgage as an individual borrower helps you determine whether you meet the necessary criteria to refinance the house in your name alone.

5. **How much equity do I currently have in the house?** Asking about the amount of equity in the house helps you understand the potential loan-to-value ratio and the options available for refinancing.

6. **Will refinancing affect the division of assets during the divorce settlement?** Inquiring about the impact of refinancing on the division of assets helps you understand whether refinancing may have implications for the overall distribution of property.

7. **Can you help me understand the terms and conditions of the refinanced mortgage?** Asking for clarification on the terms and conditions of the new mortgage helps you make an informed decision and ensure that the terms align with your financial goals.

8. **What are the potential benefits and risks of refinancing?** Inquiring about the advantages and risks associated with refinancing helps you weigh the potential benefits, such as reducing monthly payments, against any potential drawbacks or challenges.

9. **How long will the refinancing process take?** Asking about the timeline for refinancing helps you plan accordingly and ensures that the process aligns with your divorce proceedings and other time-sensitive matters.

10. **Are there any legal considerations or documentation requirements I should be aware of when refinancing during a divorce?** Inquiring about the legal aspects and documentation required during the refinancing process helps you ensure compliance with any legal requirements and avoid potential complications.

Asking these questions will help you gather important information and make informed decisions about refinancing your house during the divorce. Remember to consult with a mortgage professional or lender who specializes in divorce-related refinancing for personalized advice based on your specific situation.

Why is it so important to ask these questions about refinancing your house during a divorce?

Protect Your Financial Interests: When going through a divorce, your financial situation is likely to change significantly. By asking the right questions, you can assess the financial implications of refinancing your house and safeguard your economic well-being. Understanding the potential costs, terms, and impact on your credit will enable you to make informed choices that protect your financial interests.

1. **Clarify Ownership and Responsibility:** Refinancing your house often involves addressing questions about ownership and responsibility. Asking about how the mortgage will be handled, who will be responsible for the payments, and how the equity will be divided can prevent future disputes and ensure a fair outcome. These questions help establish clear boundaries and avoid potential complications down the line.

2. **Understand the Legal and Tax Implications:** Refinancing a house during a divorce can have legal and tax implications that must be considered. By asking about potential legal obligations, such as prepayment penalties or legal fees, you can avoid unexpected costs. Additionally, understanding the tax consequences, such as capital gains or deductions, will help you plan your finances effectively and avoid any surprises come tax season.

3. **Evaluate Financial Feasibility:** Divorce often involves dividing assets, which may affect your financial capacity to refinance your house. By asking questions related to income requirements, debt-to-income ratios, and credit scores, you can assess whether refinancing is a feasible option for you. Understanding the lending criteria and potential limitations will allow you to plan accordingly and explore alternative solutions if necessary.

4. **Seek Professional Guidance:** Refinancing a house during a divorce is a complex process that benefits from professional expertise. Asking the right questions can help you identify the need for hiring a mortgage broker, financial advisor, or attorney who specializes in divorce and real estate. Seeking professional guidance ensures that you receive accurate information, personalized advice, and necessary support throughout the refinancing journey.

10 Essential Questions to Ask a Mortgage Lender When Buying a House on Your Own Post-Divorce

Navigating the home-buying process post-divorce is an empowering yet challenging experience. For many, it's the first time they're buying a house on their own, which comes with unique financial considerations and responsibilities. A key player in this journey is your mortgage lender, who will guide you through the borrowing process. Asking the right questions can make all the difference in securing a home loan that aligns with your financial goals and stability.

1. **What mortgage options are available to me?** There are various types of mortgages—conventional, FHA, VA, and USDA loans, each with different requirements and benefits. If you're newly single, your income and credit profile may differ from what it was during your marriage. Understanding which options are available to you can help you choose a loan that fits your financial situation and long-term goals.

2. **How will my credit score affect my interest rate?** Your credit score plays a major role in determining your interest rate. Post-divorce, your credit might look different, especially if you've had to divide debts or remove your name from joint accounts. Understanding how your credit score influences your rate allows you to plan for either improvements or adjustments to your budget.

3. **What will my monthly payment be, including taxes and insurance?** It's not just the mortgage payment you need to budget for—property taxes, homeowner's insurance, and potentially mortgage insurance are part of your monthly cost. Ask for a breakdown of these costs so you're fully aware of your monthly obligations before signing anything.

4. **What are the closing costs and can they be rolled into my loan?** Closing costs can add up to 2%–5% of the loan amount. Knowing these costs upfront helps you budget accordingly. In some cases, these fees can be rolled into your mortgage, which could be helpful if your post-divorce finances are tight.

5. **Are there any first-time homebuyer or special programs available?** If this is your first time buying a home solo, you may qualify for special programs that offer lower interest rates, reduced down payments, or even grants. Knowing what's available can help you save significantly on your home purchase.

6. **Can I get pre-approved, and how long does it last?** A pre-approval not only gives you a clear picture of your borrowing power but also shows sellers that you're a serious buyer. Ask your lender how long the pre-approval is valid, as the housing market and your financial situation could change.

7. **Are there penalties for prepaying my mortgage?** If your financial situation improves and you want to pay off your mortgage faster, you'll want to know if there are any prepayment penalties. Some lenders charge fees if you pay off your loan early, and understanding these terms upfront prevents any surprises.

8. **Can I get pre-approved, and how long does it last?** A pre-approval not only gives you a clear picture of your borrowing power but also shows sellers that you're a serious buyer. Ask your lender how long the pre-approval is valid, as the housing market and your financial situation could change.

9. Are there penalties for prepaying my mortgage? If your financial situation improves and you want to pay off your mortgage faster, you'll want to know if there are any prepayment penalties. Some lenders charge fees if you pay off your loan early, and understanding these terms upfront prevents any surprises.

10. What happens if I miss a payment? Life post-divorce can come with financial unpredictability. Understanding the consequences of a missed payment, as well as your lender's policies on late fees and grace periods, can help you manage any unforeseen financial hiccups.

It's important to remember that…

Buying a house on your own after a divorce is a bold step towards reclaiming your independence and rebuilding your life. But it's crucial to go into it with eyes wide open. Asking your mortgage lender these ten questions ensures that you understand not just what you're signing up for, but how to thrive as a solo homeowner.

_____

_____

_____

_____

_____

_____

Tax Advisors

What They Do: A tax advisor helps you understand the financial implications of divorce, including how alimony, child support, and asset division affect your taxes.

Why You Need Them: Divorce changes your filing status, potential deductions, and how you handle shared assets. Getting it right can save money and prevent legal issues.

What to Say When You Reach Out: "Hi, I'm going through a divorce and need help understanding how it will affect my taxes. Can you assist with planning and filing during and after the divorce?"

What They Can Help With:

- Filing status changes

- Handling alimony and child support taxes

- Managing property and asset division

- Tax-efficient settlement strategies

- Post-divorce financial planning

10 Questions to Ask Your Tax Accountant During Your Divorce

Divorce isn't just an emotional journey—it's a financial one, too. As you untangle shared assets and start building your independent financial future, taxes often become a key consideration. From filing status changes to potential implications for alimony, child support, and property division, it's essential to understand how your divorce will affect your tax obligations. A knowledgeable tax accountant can guide you through these complexities and help you make informed decisions that protect your financial well-being.

---

1. **How will my filing status change?**

    ○ **Why it's essential:** Your tax filing status (single, married filing jointly, head of household) can significantly impact your tax bracket, deductions, and credits.

    ○ **How to ask:** "Can you explain how my tax filing status will change after my divorce and what that means for my taxes next year?"

2. **Are there tax implications for alimony or spousal support?**

    ○ **Why it's essential:** Depending on your divorce agreement, alimony payments may have tax consequences for the payer or recipient.

    ○ **How to ask:** "Will receiving or paying alimony affect my taxes, and are there specific steps I should take to plan for this?"

3. What are the tax implications of dividing marital assets?

- ○ **Why it's essential:** Transfers of property or investments as part of a divorce settlement may trigger tax liabilities.
- ○ **How to ask:** "When we divide our assets, like our home or retirement accounts, will there be any taxes I need to be aware of?"

4. Who will claim the children as dependents?

- ○ **Why it's essential:** Only one parent can claim each child as a dependent, which impacts tax credits like the Child Tax Credit or Earned Income Tax Credit.
- ○ **How to ask:** "Can you help me understand how claiming dependents works after divorce and what agreements I need to have in place?"

5. How will selling the family home affect my taxes?

- ○ **Why it's essential:** Selling a home may result in capital gains taxes, especially if it was a primary asset.
- ○ **How to ask:** "If I sell our house during or after the divorce, what are the potential tax consequences I should prepare for?"

6. What should I know about dividing retirement accounts?

- ○ **Why it's essential:** Splitting retirement accounts like IRAs or 401(k)s can trigger taxes and penalties if not done correctly.
- ○ **How to ask:** "Are there specific tax strategies or considerations for dividing retirement accounts in a divorce settlement?"

7. What changes should I make to my tax withholdings?

- ○ **Why it's essential:** Divorce often affects your income, deductions, and filing status, which may require adjustments to avoid under- or overpaying taxes.
- ○ **How to ask:** "Should I update my tax withholdings now that I'm divorced, and how do I go about doing that?"

8. Are there tax implications for child support?

- ○ **Why it's essential:** Unlike alimony, child support payments are generally not tax-deductible or taxable, but it's crucial to understand the rules.
- ○ **How to ask:** "Does child support impact my taxes in any way, and do I need to document these payments for tax purposes?"

9. Will I be eligible for any new deductions or credits?

- ○ **Why it's essential:** Your financial situation after divorce may make you eligible for tax benefits like the Earned Income Tax Credit or education-related deductions.
- ○ **How to ask:** "Now that I'm divorced, are there any new tax credits or deductions I might qualify for?"

10. What records should I keep for future tax filings?

- ○ **Why it's essential:** Proper documentation is essential for accurately filing taxes and avoiding audits.
- ○ **How to ask:** "What financial and legal records should I hold onto after the divorce, and for how long?"

Asking these critical questions can help you navigate the tax-related complexities of divorce with confidence. Your tax accountant is there to guide you through the process, ensuring your financial transition is as smooth as possible.

Remember, each divorce situation is unique, and these tips may not apply to every case. It's crucial to consult with professionals who can provide tailored advice based on your specific circumstances.

Children's Therapists

What They Do: A children's therapist provides emotional and psychological support to kids experiencing the effects of divorce. They help children understand and process the changes happening within their family, offering coping mechanisms and emotional validation.

Why You Need Them: Divorce can be confusing and distressing for children. A therapist helps them navigate their feelings, express themselves safely, and build emotional resilience during this transition.

What to Say When You Reach Out: "Hi, my child is experiencing emotional challenges due to our divorce, and I'm looking for a therapist who specializes in family transitions. Can you explain how you support children through divorce-related issues?"

What They Can Help With:

- Helping children express emotions healthily

- Building coping mechanisms for family changes

- Managing feelings of confusion, sadness, or anger

- Addressing behavioral changes due to family restructuring

- Providing a safe space for kids to talk about their experiences

10 Essential Questions To Ask A Children's Therapist

Divorce is not only challenging for you but also for your children. Kids often struggle to understand the changes in their family dynamics, and they may experience feelings of confusion, sadness, anger, or anxiety. A children's therapist can provide the support they need to process these emotions in a healthy way. Finding the right therapist is crucial to ensuring your child feels safe, heard, and understood. Here are 10 essential questions to ask a potential children's therapist to determine if they are the right fit for your family during this transition.

1. **What is your experience working with children navigating divorce?** Divorce-specific therapy requires an understanding of how children process grief, conflict, and big changes. A therapist experienced with divorce-related family dynamics can address concerns like loyalty conflicts, communication with both parents, and changes in routine.

   Follow-Up Questions:

   ◦ How many children have you worked with who were experiencing parental divorce?
   ◦ Are you familiar with addressing custody-related anxiety?
   ◦ Have you supported children through high-conflict divorces?

2. What therapeutic approaches do you use with children?
Different coaches have different philosophies. Some are solution-focused, while others are more emotionally driven. It's important to understand whether their approach matches your communication style and family needs.

Follow-Up Questions:

- Do you use play therapy, CBT, or art therapy?
- How do you decide which method is best for each child?
- Are parents involved in some sessions to support the child's healing?

3. How do you help children express their feelings about divorce?
One of the biggest challenges in co-parenting is communication. A good coach provides tools and strategies for clear, conflict-free discussions about your children.

Follow-Up Questions:

- Do you use creative methods like drawing or storytelling?
- How do you encourage children to talk about their worries or fears?
- Are there specific activities designed to help with emotional expression?

4. How do you handle situations where a child is resistant to therapy? Not all children are open to therapy right away. Understanding how the therapist manages resistance can help you gauge their patience and skill in building trust.

Follow-Up Questions:

- What strategies do you use to make children feel comfortable?
- How long does it typically take for children to open up?
- Do you involve parents if a child is resistant?

Find the Experts you need at freshstartsregistry.com/experts

5. **How do you communicate with parents about their child's progress?** It's crucial to stay informed about your child's emotional well-being during therapy. Knowing how the therapist updates parents helps you feel connected to your child's progress.

Follow-Up Questions:

- Do you provide regular updates or progress reports?
- Are parents included in sessions occasionally?
- How do you handle privacy and confidentiality?

6. **Are you experienced with co-parenting situations and blended families?** Divorce often includes co-parenting challenges or the introduction of blended families. A therapist familiar with these dynamics can help your child adjust and express their feelings constructively.

Follow-Up Questions:

- Have you worked with children who split time between two households?
- Do you provide support for children adjusting to blended families?
- How do you manage situations where parents have conflicting parenting styles?

7. **Are your sessions in-person, virtual, or both?** Flexibility matters, especially if you're managing shared custody or living in different locations. Knowing the therapist's availability can help you plan for consistent care.

Follow-Up Questions:

- Do you offer virtual sessions if in-person is not possible?
- Are weekend or after-school appointments available?
- Can you accommodate fluctuating schedules due to custody arrangements?

8. **What are your fees, and how are they structured?** Therapy can be a long-term commitment, and understanding the costs upfront helps you plan accordingly. Ask about insurance, session costs, and payment plans.

   Follow-Up Questions:

   - Do you accept insurance, or is it private pay only?
   - Are there package deals for multiple sessions?
   - What is your cancellation or rescheduling policy?

9. **How do you help children navigate loyalty conflicts and communication issues between parents?** Divorce sometimes places children in the middle of conflict, leading to loyalty struggles and communication challenges. A skilled therapist can help them navigate these feelings without guilt or anxiety.

   Follow-Up Questions:

   - Do you address loyalty conflicts directly with the child?
   - How do you handle situations where children feel stuck between parents?
   - Can you mediate discussions to help children express their feelings safely?

10. **Can you provide references or testimonials from parents of children you've worked with?** Hearing from other parents about their child's progress and the therapist's approach can help you feel confident in your decision. Testimonials provide real-world insights into the therapist's impact.

    Follow-Up Questions:

    - Can you share testimonials from families you've worked with?
    - Are there references I can contact?
    - Do you have success stories of helping children transition through divorce?

It's important to remember that…

Finding the right therapist for your child during a divorce is one of the most supportive things you can do for their emotional health. The right professional will help them express their feelings, navigate family changes, and build resilience in a safe environment. By asking these ten essential questions, you can be confident that the therapist you choose is skilled, compassionate, and equipped to handle the unique challenges your child may face.

Career Coaches

What They Do: A career coach helps you navigate career changes that may arise due to divorce, whether you're re-entering the workforce, changing jobs, or seeking financial independence.

Why You Need Them: Divorce can change your financial situation and career needs. A coach can help you rebuild your professional identity and increase your income.

What to Say When You Reach Out: "Hi, I'm navigating a career transition due to my divorce. I need guidance on finding job opportunities and building a professional plan. How can you assist with this process?"

What They Can Help With:

- Identifying career opportunities
- Building a new professional identity
- Resume and interview preparation
- Finding flexible work arrangements
- Rebuilding financial independence

10 Reasons to Work with a Career Coach During Your Divorce Process

Divorce can be a challenging and emotionally turbulent experience that impacts every facet of your life, including your career. Amidst the overwhelming emotions and practicalities of untangling a shared life, it's easy to overlook the significance of maintaining or reshaping your professional identity during this difficult transition. This is where a career coach can provide invaluable support, guidance, and encouragement, helping you navigate the complex intersection between personal upheaval and professional aspirations. We rounded up 10 reasons why it's crucial to work with a career coach during your divorce, and we'll delve into why it is essential to consider partnering with a career coach during a divorce, and how their expertise can empower you to embrace new opportunities, rebuild your confidence, and forge a fulfilling career path that aligns with your post-divorce life goals.

1. Career exploration and assessment: A career coach can help you explore your skills, strengths, and interests to identify new career possibilities that align with your passions and goals

2. Resume and job search support: A career coach can assist you in updating your resume, developing job search strategies, and navigating the job market to enhance your chances of finding suitable employment.

3. Skill development: If you need to acquire new skills or enhance existing ones, a career coach can provide guidance on relevant training programs or professional development opportunities to boost your marketability.

4. Building confidence and self-esteem: Going through a divorce can often impact one's confidence and self-esteem. A career coach can help you rebuild your self-assurance and provide support as you navigate career transitions and challenges.

5. Setting career goals: A career coach can help you set realistic and achievable career goals, taking into account your personal circumstances, interests, and aspirations.

6. Networking and professional connections: A career coach can guide you in expanding your professional network, connecting with industry contacts, and leveraging relationships to uncover job opportunities or gain valuable insights.

7. Interview preparation and skills: A career coach can assist you in preparing for interviews, offering guidance on effective communication, presentation, and interview techniques to help you make a positive impression on potential employers.

8. Entrepreneurship and business guidance: If you are considering starting your own business or pursuing self-employment, a career coach can provide guidance on entrepreneurship, helping you navigate the process and develop a viable business plan.

9. Negotiating job offers and salary: A career coach can provide guidance on negotiating job offers and salary, ensuring that you secure fair compensation and favorable terms in your new role.

10. Balancing work and personal life: A career coach can help you establish a healthy work-life balance, ensuring that your career decisions and commitments align with your personal well-being and priorities during and after the divorce process.

Working with a career coach during the divorce process can provide valuable support, guidance, and resources to help you navigate career transitions, identify new opportunities, and regain confidence in your professional life. They can help you develop a strategic plan for your career, enhance your job search skills, and create a fulfilling and successful career path moving forward.

10 Essential Questions to Ask a Career Coach

Divorce is a life-altering event that often affects every aspect of your life, including your career. For many, it can be a time to reassess professional goals, re-enter the workforce, or pivot into a more financially independent role. A career coach can provide the clarity, strategy, and confidence needed to make empowered decisions during this transition. But how do you find the right coach? Here are 10 essential questions to ask a potential career coach to ensure they're the right fit for your divorce journey.

1. **What is your experience working with clients going through divorce?** Divorce comes with unique challenges like financial shifts, emotional stress, and potential gaps in employment. A coach experienced in divorce-related career transitions understands the complexities of re-entering the workforce, changing careers, or negotiating salaries during a life shift.

   Follow-Up Questions:

   - How many clients have you coached who were navigating divorce?
   - Are you familiar with the financial pressures divorce can bring?
   - Have you helped clients re-establish careers after long gaps?

2. **How do you help clients identify career goals post-divorce?** Your goals may look different after a divorce. A good coach can help you redefine what success looks like, align your career path with your new life, and set achievable milestones.

   Follow-Up Questions:

   - Do you use career assessments or goal-setting frameworks?
   - How do you help clients discover strengths and skills they may have overlooked?
   - Can you help with goal-setting for both short-term and long-term career plans?

3. **What strategies do you use to help clients re-enter the workforce?** If you've been out of the workforce for years, re-entry can feel daunting. A career coach should have proven strategies for updating your resume, building confidence, and networking effectively.

   Follow-Up Questions:

   - How do you help clients address employment gaps?
   - Do you provide guidance on resume building and LinkedIn optimization?
   - What networking strategies do you recommend?

4. **How do you help clients build financial independence through career choices?** Divorce often shifts financial responsibilities. A career coach should understand how to help you move toward financial independence through smart career choices and salary negotiations.

   Follow-Up Questions:

   - Can you help with salary negotiation strategies?
   - Do you offer guidance on high-demand career paths?
   - How do you support clients in building long-term financial stability?

Find the Experts you need at freshstartsregistry.com/experts

5. **Do you offer support for career pivots and changing industries?**
For some, divorce is a catalyst for change—not just personally, but professionally. If you're considering a career pivot, a coach experienced in industry changes can guide you smoothly through the transition.

Follow-Up Questions:

- Have you helped clients successfully change industries?
- Do you provide guidance for skill development or certification programs?
- How do you assess transferable skills?

6. **Are your coaching sessions in-person, virtual, or both?** Divorce often brings logistical challenges—like new living arrangements or custody schedules—that can impact your availability. A coach offering virtual sessions provides greater flexibility.

Follow-Up Questions:

- Do you offer evening or weekend sessions?
- Are virtual sessions available if I'm unable to meet in person?
- Is there support for quick questions or check-ins between sessions?

7. **How do you help clients overcome self-doubt and build confidence?** Divorce can shake your confidence, especially if you've been out of the workforce or financially dependent. A career coach should be skilled at helping you rebuild self-assurance and overcome imposter syndrome.

Follow-Up Questions:

- Do you offer mindset and confidence-building exercises?
- How do you handle clients who struggle with self-doubt?
- What tools do you use to boost career confidence?

8. **What are your fees, and how are they structured?** Understanding the cost structure is crucial for planning, especially if you're adjusting to a new financial situation post-divorce. Some coaches charge hourly rates, while others offer packages.

   Follow-Up Questions:

   - Do you charge per session, or do you offer bundled packages?
   - Are there additional costs for resume reviews or networking events?
   - What is your cancellation or rescheduling policy?

9. **Do you help with interview preparation and job search strategies?** Landing a new role or transitioning to a better one requires polished interview skills and strategic job searching. A coach should provide mock interviews, networking strategies, and application guidance.

   Follow-Up Questions:

   - Do you offer mock interviews and feedback?
   - How do you help with tailoring resumes for specific roles?
   - What job search strategies do you recommend for hidden job markets?

10. **Can you provide references or testimonials from past clients?** References and testimonials give you insight into the coach's effectiveness and communication style. Speaking to past clients can confirm if their coaching truly delivers results.

   Follow-Up Questions:

   - Can you share success stories of clients who re-entered the workforce after divorce?
   - Do you have testimonials that reflect your support during life transitions?
   - Are there clients I can reach out to for direct feedback?

It's important to remember that...

Navigating your career during a divorce is an opportunity for reinvention and financial empowerment. The right career coach can provide clarity, strategy, and support, helping you build confidence and achieve your professional goals. By asking these ten essential questions, you ensure that your coach is not only experienced but also aligned with your unique journey and aspirations.

_____

_____

_____

_____

_____

_____

_____

_____

_____

_____

Self Help Coaches
(Mindfulness or Empowerment Coach)

What They Do: A self-help or empowerment coach helps you regain confidence, focus on personal growth, and navigate the emotional aspects of starting over.

Why You Need Them: Divorce can feel disempowering. A coach helps you reclaim your sense of identity and set meaningful personal goals.

What to Say When You Reach Out: "Hi, I'm looking for support to rebuild my life and find confidence after divorce. Can you help me focus on personal growth and self-empowerment?"

What They Can Help With:

- Building self-esteem

- Setting personal goals

- Managing stress through mindfulness

- Creating routines for emotional well-being

- Rediscovering identity beyond marriage

10 Essential Questions to Ask a Life Coach While Navigating a Divorce

Divorce is a life-altering event that often affects every aspect of your life, including your career. For many, it can be a time to reassess professional goals, re-enter the workforce, or pivot into a more financially independent role. A career coach can provide the clarity, strategy, and confidence needed to make empowered decisions during this transition. But how do you find the right coach? Here are 10 essential questions to ask a potential career coach to ensure they're the right fit for your divorce journey.

1. **What is your experience working with clients going through divorce?** Divorce is uniquely challenging and impacts multiple aspects of life—emotionally, financially, and socially. A life coach experienced in divorce-specific coaching understands the complexities involved and can provide tailored strategies for moving forward.

   Follow-Up Questions:

   - How many clients have you coached through a divorce?
   - Are you familiar with the emotional challenges specific to divorce?
   - Have you worked with clients transitioning from married life to singlehood?

2. **What areas of life do you focus on during coaching?** Life coaching can cover many areas, including emotional healing, financial stability, goal setting, and personal growth. Understanding the coach's areas of expertise helps you determine if they align with your needs.

Follow-Up Questions:

- Do you focus more on emotional recovery, practical planning, or both?
- How do you help clients rebuild confidence after a major life change?
- Can you help with setting financial and career goals post-divorce?

3. **How do you help clients redefine their identity after divorce?** Divorce often disrupts your sense of identity, especially if you've been married for many years. A skilled life coach can guide you through redefining who you are outside of the relationship.

Follow-Up Questions:

- Do you use specific exercises or tools for identity rebuilding?
- How do you help clients discover their passions and strengths?
- What strategies do you use to rebuild self-worth and confidence?

4. **What strategies do you use to help clients manage stress and anxiety during divorce?** Divorce is emotionally taxing, and stress levels can be overwhelming. A good life coach will provide coping mechanisms and mindfulness techniques to help you manage anxiety and build resilience.

Follow-Up Questions:

- Do you incorporate mindfulness or stress-relief practices into coaching?
- How do you help clients handle anxiety related to financial or custody issues?
- Do you offer guidance for managing conflict with an ex-spouse?

Find the Experts you need at freshstartsregistry.com/experts

5. **How do you support clients in setting goals for their new chapter?** One of the most empowering aspects of working with a life coach is setting clear, achievable goals for your next chapter. This could include career ambitions, personal development, or creating new routines.

   Follow-Up Questions:

   - Do you use structured goal-setting frameworks?
   - How do you help clients prioritize their goals?
   - Can you assist with both short-term and long-term planning?

6. **Are your coaching sessions in-person, virtual, or both?** Flexibility is crucial during a life transition like divorce, especially if you are managing new schedules, moving, or adjusting to co-parenting arrangements.

   Follow-Up Questions:

   - Do you offer evening or weekend sessions?
   - Are virtual sessions available if I'm unable to meet in person?
   - Is there support for quick questions or check-ins between sessions?

7. **How do you measure progress during coaching?** It's important to know how your progress will be tracked. A coach who provides clear milestones and regularly evaluates your growth can help keep you accountable and motivated.

   Follow-Up Questions:

   - Do you set specific goals and track progress against them?
   - How do you adjust coaching plans if goals are not being met?
   - Do you provide progress updates after each session?

8. **What are your fees, and how are they structured?** Understanding the cost structure is crucial, especially if your finances are shifting during a divorce. Some coaches charge per session, while others offer packages.

Follow-Up Questions:

- Do you charge per session, or do you offer bundled packages?
- Are there additional costs for worksheets or personalized plans?
- What is your cancellation or rescheduling policy?

9. **Do you offer guidance for rebuilding social networks and community after divorce?** Divorce can significantly impact your social circle. A good life coach will help you rebuild your support network, find new communities, and regain confidence in social settings.

Follow-Up Questions:

- Do you help clients find new social outlets after divorce?
- Can you provide strategies for rebuilding friendships and community connections?
- How do you help clients address loneliness and isolation?

10. **Can you provide references or testimonials from past clients?** Testimonials and references provide real-world proof of a coach's effectiveness and style. Speaking with past clients can help you understand if the coach's approach aligns with your needs.

Follow-Up Questions:

- Can you share testimonials from clients who navigated divorce?
- Are there clients I can speak with for direct feedback?
- Do you have success stories of clients who transformed their lives post-divorce?

It's important to remember that...

Working with a life coach during a divorce can be transformative, offering you the clarity, resilience, and confidence needed to move forward. By asking these ten essential questions, you ensure that your life coach is not only experienced but also aligned with your personal growth, healing, and future goals. Finding the right coach can help you thrive, not just survive, through this transition.

_____

_____

_____

_____

_____

_____

_____

_____

_____

_____

Professional Organizers

What They Do: A home organizer helps you sort through belongings, downsize, and set up a new space that reflects your new life after divorce.

Why You Need Them: Divorce often involves moving or reconfiguring shared spaces. An organizer helps reduce clutter and create a fresh start.

What to Say When You Reach Out: "Hi, I'm moving after my divorce and need help organizing and downsizing my belongings. Do you specialize in transitions like this?"

What They Can Help With:

- Sorting and decluttering shared items
- Creating an organized new living space
- Reducing emotional overwhelm related to belongings
- Preparing for moving or selling the marital home
- Establishing routines in a new home

10 Essential Questions to Ask a Professional Organizer

Divorce often means not just an emotional reset but also a physical one. You may be moving, downsizing, or reimagining your living space entirely. A professional organizer can help simplify this transition by decluttering, organizing, and setting up new systems that bring peace and clarity to your life. Whether you are staying in the marital home or starting fresh somewhere new, the right professional organizer can make this process much less overwhelming. Here are 10 essential questions to ask a potential professional organizer to ensure they're the right fit for your post-divorce journey.

1. **What is your experience working with clients going through a divorce?** Divorce-related organizing is different from general decluttering. Emotions run high, and decisions about shared belongings can be complex. An organizer experienced in divorce transitions will understand the emotional and logistical hurdles involved.

   Follow-Up Questions:

   - How many clients have you worked with who were transitioning after divorce?
   - Are you familiar with splitting household items and decluttering sentimental belongings?
   - Have you handled projects involving downsizing or moving post-divorce?

2. **What is your process for helping clients decide what to keep, sell, or donate?** Divorce often means splitting possessions and making hard decisions about what stays and what goes. A well-structured process for sorting can make this less emotional and more strategic.

   Follow-Up Questions:

   - Do you have a specific method for sorting belongings?
   - How do you manage disagreements over shared items?
   - Can you help facilitate donations, sales, or consignment of items?

3. **How do you handle sentimental items that are difficult to let go of?** Divorce often brings up emotional attachment to belongings. A skilled organizer should have compassion and strategies for helping you navigate decisions around sentimental items.

   Follow-Up Questions:

   - Do you help clients work through emotional attachments?
   - How do you approach organizing keepsakes and heirlooms?
   - Can you help with creating memory boxes or storage solutions?

4. **Are you experienced with moving and downsizing services?** If you are relocating or downsizing, a professional organizer can help streamline the process, manage logistics, and reduce stress.

   Follow-Up Questions:

   - Do you offer packing and unpacking services?
   - Can you coordinate with moving companies?
   - How do you handle organizing in smaller spaces after downsizing?
   -

5. **How do you handle shared spaces when both parties still live in the home?** Sometimes, divorcing couples stay under the same roof during the transition. An organizer familiar with this situation can create boundaries, organize shared spaces, and reduce conflict.

Follow-Up Questions:

- Have you organized for families navigating divorce while cohabitating?
- How do you help create separate living spaces within the same home?
- Can you assist with privacy-focused organization?

6. **Are your organizing sessions in-person, virtual, or both?** Flexibility is important, especially if you're coordinating around custody schedules, moving timelines, or emotional readiness.

Follow-Up Questions:

- Do you offer virtual organizing sessions?
- Are evening or weekend appointments available?
- Can you provide support for organizing both in-person and remotely?

7. **Do you provide systems for long-term organization and maintenance?** The real value of professional organizing is in creating systems that last. A good organizer will not only declutter but also implement sustainable solutions for your new life.

Follow-Up Questions:

- Do you create customized systems for ongoing organization?
- How do you help clients maintain their space after the initial project?
- Do you offer follow-up sessions to ensure the systems are working?

8. What are your fees, and how are they structured? Understanding the cost structure upfront helps you budget accordingly. Some organizers charge hourly rates, while others offer packages for larger projects.

Follow-Up Questions:

- Do you charge by the hour or per project?
- Are there package deals for whole-home organizing or downsizing?
- What is your cancellation policy?

9. Can you help with digital organizing as well?
Divorce isn't just about physical items. You may need help sorting through digital records, photos, and documents that need to be organized or shared.

Follow-Up Questions:

- Do you assist with organizing digital files and photos?
- Can you help streamline important divorce-related documents?
- Are you experienced with setting up secure digital storage?

10. Can you provide references or testimonials from past clients?
Hearing from past clients can give you insights into their approach, professionalism, and ability to handle divorce-related transitions smoothly.

Follow-Up Questions:

- Can you share testimonials from clients who were going through a divorce?
- Are you able to provide references for recent projects?
- Do you have success stories of major downsizing or post-divorce moves?

Find the Experts you need at freshstartsregistry.com/experts

It's important to remember that...

Navigating the physical changes of divorce—whether it's downsizing, decluttering, or moving—can be incredibly challenging. The right professional organizer not only helps streamline the process but also brings peace of mind and clarity to your new space. By asking these ten essential questions, you ensure that your organizer is not only experienced but also empathetic and skilled at handling the unique challenges of divorce.

_____

_____

_____

_____

_____

_____

_____

_____

_____

Fitness/Movement Coaches

What They Do: A fitness or movement coach helps you rebuild physical strength, manage stress, and restore confidence through tailored exercise programs. They can work with you to create routines that fit your new lifestyle and provide a healthy outlet for the emotional challenges of divorce.

Why You Need Them: Divorce is emotionally draining, and physical movement is a proven way to reduce stress, combat anxiety, and rebuild confidence. A fitness coach can help you reestablish healthy routines, improve your mental well-being, and regain physical strength during a challenging time.

What to Say When You Reach Out: "Hi, I'm going through a divorce and looking to establish a fitness routine to manage stress and improve my health. Do you specialize in working with clients going through life transitions like divorce?"

What They Can Help With:

- Creating personalized workout plans

- Managing stress and anxiety through movement

- Building strength and confidence

- Establishing a self-care routine

- Encouraging physical and mental resilience

10 Essential Questions to Ask a Fitness Instructor or Movement Coach

Divorce is not just an emotional transition—it's a physical one, too. Stress, anxiety, and emotional upheaval can take a toll on your body, affecting your sleep, energy levels, and overall health. A fitness instructor or movement coach can be a powerful ally during this time, helping you rebuild strength, boost confidence, and release stress through physical activity. But finding the right fit is crucial. Here are 10 essential questions to ask a potential fitness instructor or movement coach while navigating your divorce to ensure they align with your needs and goals.

1. **What is your experience working with clients navigating life transitions like divorce?** Divorce can come with heightened emotional stress and sometimes physical health changes. A fitness coach who understands the complexities of life transitions can design a workout plan that not only focuses on physical strength but also emotional well-being.

   Follow-Up Questions:

   - How many clients have you trained who were going through major life changes?
   - Do you incorporate stress relief and mindfulness into your programs?
   - Are you familiar with gentle re-entry for people who haven't exercised in a while?

2. **What type of fitness programs do you offer? (Strength, cardio, yoga, etc.)** Everyone's fitness needs are different. Some may need strength training to feel empowered, while others might benefit from yoga or Pilates for mindfulness and relaxation. Understanding their offerings helps you choose the right kind of support.

Follow-Up Questions:

   ◦ Do you offer customized workout plans?
   ◦ Are there options for low-impact workouts if I'm recovering from stress or injury?
   ◦ Can you help with both weight training and mindfulness-based movement?

3. **Do you offer one-on-one sessions, group classes, or both?** The setting of your fitness routine matters. Some people thrive in group environments, while others prefer the privacy and focused attention of one-on-one coaching.

Follow-Up Questions:

   ◦ Are private sessions available if I'm not comfortable in a group setting?
   ◦ Do you offer virtual classes if I'm unable to travel?
   ◦ Can you provide hybrid options, mixing group classes and personal training?

4. **How do you help clients set and achieve fitness goals?** During a divorce, goal-setting can feel overwhelming. A fitness instructor with structured plans and realistic milestones can make your fitness journey empowering rather than intimidating.

Follow-Up Questions:

   ◦ Do you create customized fitness plans based on individual goals?
   ◦ How do you measure progress?
   ◦ Do you offer support for setting realistic expectations during challenging times?

Find the Experts you need at freshstartsregistry.com/experts

5. How do you handle emotional days when motivation is low?
Divorce can be an emotional rollercoaster, and there will be days
when getting out of bed—let alone working out—feels impossible. A
compassionate coach knows how to motivate without judgment.

Follow-Up Questions:

- How do you help clients stay consistent when they're
  emotionally drained?
- Do you adjust workouts based on energy levels and mood?
- Can you provide mental health check-ins during sessions?

**6. Are you experienced with trauma-informed fitness or movement
therapy?** Divorce can sometimes be accompanied by emotional
trauma. A coach experienced in trauma-informed movement is
sensitive to triggers and ensures that physical activity is safe and
supportive.

Follow-Up Questions:

- Are you trained in trauma-sensitive fitness approaches?
- Do you understand how to work with clients who may have
  anxiety or PTSD?
- How do you create a safe and welcoming environment during
  sessions?

7. Are your sessions in-person, virtual, or both? Flexibility matters
during a divorce transition, especially if you are moving, handling
childcare, or adjusting to a new routine. A coach who offers both
virtual and in-person options can keep you consistent.

Follow-Up Questions:

- Do you offer virtual training sessions?
- Are there flexible scheduling options like evenings or
  weekends?
- Can you accommodate travel or relocation by switching to
  virtual sessions?

8. What are your fees, and how are they structured?
Understanding the cost upfront helps you budget during a potentially financially sensitive time. Some coaches charge hourly, while others offer packages.s.

Follow-Up Questions:

- Do you charge per session or offer package deals?
- Are there discounts for long-term commitments or multiple sessions per week?
- What is your cancellation policy?

9. Do you provide nutritional guidance or partner with a nutritionist? Exercise is only part of the wellness equation—nutrition plays a huge role in emotional and physical health. A coach who offers nutritional guidance can help you fuel your body for strength and recovery.

Follow-Up Questions:

- Do you provide meal planning or nutrition tips?
- Are you partnered with nutritionists for holistic support?
- Can you help with stress-related eating habits?

10. Can you provide references or testimonials from past clients?
Hearing about other clients' experiences, especially those who were navigating major life changes, can give you confidence in your decision. Testimonials can also offer insight into the coach's style and effectiveness.

Follow-Up Questions:

- Can you share testimonials from clients who were going through divorce?
- Do you have before-and-after stories that showcase progress?
- Are there clients I can speak with directly for feedback?

It's important to remember that...

Divorce is a transformative journey, and taking care of your body is a vital part of healing. The right fitness instructor or movement coach helps you rebuild physical strength, reduce emotional stress, and find confidence as you step into your new chapter. By asking these ten essential questions, you can find a coach who not only understands fitness but also the emotional weight of starting over.

_____

_____

_____

_____

_____

_____

_____

_____

_____

Relationship Coaches

What They Do: A relationship coach helps you understand and heal from the relationship dynamics that led to divorce. They guide you through processing past relationship patterns, setting healthy boundaries, and preparing for future connections— whether that's co-parenting with your ex or building new relationships post-divorce.

Why You Need Them: Divorce is often an opportunity for deep personal growth and self-discovery. A relationship coach helps you identify patterns, heal emotional wounds, and create healthier dynamics moving forward. If you are co-parenting, they can also help you navigate communication with your ex in a constructive way.

What to Say When You Reach Out: "Hi, I'm going through a divorce and would like support in understanding my relationship patterns and healing from this experience. Do you specialize in divorce recovery and co-parenting dynamics?"

What They Can Help With:

- Understanding relationship patterns and triggers
- Healing from emotional wounds
- Setting healthy boundaries with your ex
- Preparing for new, healthier relationships
- Effective communication for co-parenting

10 Essential Questions to Ask a Relationship Coach

Divorce often brings about profound shifts in how we understand relationships—not just with our former partners, but with ourselves, family members, and friends. A relationship coach can help you process the end of your marriage, heal emotional wounds, and learn how to build healthier connections moving forward. Whether you want to improve communication with your ex for co-parenting, or simply rebuild your confidence for future relationships, the right coach can be a transformative ally. Here are 10 essential questions to ask a potential relationship coach while navigating your divorce to ensure they're the right fit for your healing journey.

1. **What is your experience working with clients going through divorce?** Divorce-specific relationship coaching requires an understanding of grief, communication challenges, co-parenting dynamics, and emotional healing. A coach experienced in divorce transitions will know how to address these issues with empathy and practical strategies.

   Follow-Up Questions:

   ◦ How many clients have you worked with during or after divorce?
   ◦ Are you familiar with helping clients manage co-parenting dynamics?
   ◦ Do you have experience with high-conflict divorce situations?

2. **What is your coaching philosophy and approach?** Different relationship coaches use different methods—some are more solution-focused, while others are reflective and emotionally driven. Understanding their coaching style helps you decide if it aligns with your personal growth journey.

Follow-Up Questions:

- Do you use a structured approach or is it more fluid based on client needs?
- Do you focus more on emotional healing, communication skills, or future relationships?
- How do you handle conflict resolution?

3. **How do you help clients rebuild trust and confidence after a divorce?** Divorce can shatter your sense of trust—not just in others, but in yourself. A good coach can help you rebuild confidence, reframe your perspective on relationships, and regain trust in your decision-making.

Follow-Up Questions:

- Do you provide exercises to rebuild self-trust and confidence?
- How do you support clients in identifying and overcoming trust issues?
- Can you help with setting boundaries in future relationships?

4. **Do you help clients improve communication with their ex for co-parenting?** If you have children, maintaining respectful and clear communication with your ex is crucial. A coach who specializes in communication strategies can make co-parenting smoother and less stressful.

Follow-Up Questions:

- Do you provide communication strategies specifically for co-parenting?
- How do you handle high-conflict communication?
- Can you help with setting up co-parenting agreements and expectations?

Find the Experts you need at freshstartsregistry.com/experts

5. **How do you handle emotionally triggering topics during coaching?** Divorce often brings up deeply painful feelings. A good relationship coach will know how to navigate sensitive topics with empathy and a focus on healing rather than re-traumatizing.

   Follow-Up Questions:

   - Are you trained in trauma-sensitive coaching?
   - How do you handle clients who become overwhelmed during sessions?
   - Do you provide tools for managing anxiety and emotional triggers?

6. **Are you experienced with helping clients enter new relationships post-divorce?** For many, divorce marks the beginning of a new chapter. If you're considering dating again, a coach experienced in relationship-building can help you navigate new dynamics with clarity and confidence.

   Follow-Up Questions:

   - Do you provide support for dating after divorce?
   - How do you help clients identify healthy relationship patterns?
   - Can you assist with setting boundaries and clear expectations in new relationships?

7. **Are your coaching sessions in-person, virtual, or both?** Flexibility matters, especially if you're adjusting to a new schedule, shared custody, or a change in location. A coach who offers virtual options can help maintain consistency.

   Follow-Up Questions:

   - Do you offer virtual coaching sessions?
   - Are evening or weekend appointments available?
   - Can you provide support if I travel or relocate?

8. **What are your fees, and how are they structured?** Understanding the cost upfront is essential for planning. Some coaches charge hourly, while others offer monthly packages or bundled sessions.

Follow-Up Questions:

- Do you charge per session or offer packages?
- Are there discounts for long-term coaching commitments?
- What is your cancellation or rescheduling policy?

9. **Do you provide actionable strategies and homework between sessions?** The effectiveness of coaching often depends on what you do between sessions. Coaches who provide homework, reflection exercises, or communication strategies keep you actively engaged in the healing process.

Follow-Up Questions:

- Do you provide exercises for personal growth and reflection?
- How do you measure progress between sessions?
- Are there follow-up tasks to reinforce what we learn?

10. **Can you provide references or testimonials from parents of children you've worked with?** Hearing from others who have worked with the coach—especially those navigating divorce—can give you confidence in their methods and empathy. Testimonials can offer insight into the coach's effectiveness and communication style.

Follow-Up Questions:

- Can you share testimonials from clients who went through divorce?
- Are there clients I can contact for feedback?
- Do you have stories of clients who successfully rebuilt relationships?

It's important to remember that...

Navigating relationships during and after a divorce can be incredibly complex. The right relationship coach not only helps you process the end of your marriage but also empowers you to rebuild confidence, improve communication, and step confidently into new relationships. By asking these ten essential questions, you can find a coach who is not only experienced but deeply understanding of the emotional complexities that come with starting over.

_____

_____

_____

_____

_____

_____

_____

_____

_____

_____

Additional Questions

10 Questions to Ask Your Insurance Broker During Your Divorce

Divorce is a life-changing event that impacts every aspect of your life, including your insurance needs. From health coverage to auto policies, it's crucial to ensure that your insurance plans reflect your new reality and provide the protection you and your family require. Navigating these changes can feel overwhelming, but having the right guidance makes all the difference.

That's where your insurance broker comes in. Asking the right questions during this transition can help you identify gaps in coverage, understand your options, and set yourself up for a secure future. Here are 10 essential questions to ask your insurance broker during your divorce to help you make informed decisions and protect what matters most.

---

1. How will my health insurance coverage change after the divorce?

- **Why it's essential:** Your tax filing status (single, married filing jointly, head of household) can significantly impact your tax bracket, deductions, and credits.

- **How to ask:** "My current health insurance is through my spouse's plan. What steps should I take to ensure I have continuous coverage after the divorce?"

2. Do I need to update my life insurance policy beneficiaries?

- ○ **Why it's essential:** Divorce often necessitates changing beneficiaries to ensure your life insurance payout aligns with your new circumstances and intentions.
- ○ **How to ask:** "Can you walk me through updating the beneficiaries on my life insurance policy? Are there any restrictions I should be aware of due to the divorce?"

3. What changes do I need to make to my homeowner's or renter's insurance?

- ○ **Why it's essential:** If you're moving out of your marital home or your living arrangements are changing, you'll need to update your insurance policies to reflect your new residence.
- ○ **How to ask:** "I'm moving to a new place after the divorce. What adjustments should I make to my current homeowner's or renter's insurance policy?"

4. Should I modify my auto insurance policy?

- ○ **Why it's essential:** If you or your spouse owned joint auto insurance, you'll need separate policies to cover your individual vehicles.
- ○ **How to ask:** "What's the process for splitting a joint auto insurance policy, and how can I ensure I maintain adequate coverage on my vehicle?"

5. Do I need additional coverage for child custody arrangements?

- ○ **Why it's essential:** If your divorce includes shared custody, consider whether your current policies adequately cover your children's needs in both households.
- ○ **How to ask:** "Do I need to adjust my policies to ensure my children are covered when they're in my care? Are there special considerations for custody arrangements?"

6. What changes should I make to my disability insurance?

- ○ **Why it's essential:** If you relied on a spouse for financial support, disability insurance can protect your income in case of an unforeseen event.
- ○ **How to ask:** "Should I revisit my disability insurance now that I'm single? What coverage level would be appropriate for my situation?"

7. Do I need umbrella insurance?

- ○ **Why it's essential:** Divorce can introduce new financial risks, and umbrella insurance offers additional liability coverage beyond standard policies.
- ○ **How to ask:** "Would umbrella insurance be beneficial for me now that I'm managing my finances independently? What does it typically cover?"
- ○

8. How can I ensure I'm adequately covered for future changes?

- ○ **Why it's essential:** Life after divorce often involves significant changes, such as career shifts or purchasing a new home. Planning ahead with your insurance broker can save you stress later.
- ○ **How to ask:** "What recommendations do you have for ensuring my insurance policies remain adaptable to future life changes?"

9. Are there discounts or adjustments available based on my new circumstances?

- ○ **Why it's essential:** Dividing finances after a divorce can be tight, so finding savings on insurance premiums is a helpful step toward managing your budget.
- ○ **How to ask:** "Are there any discounts or policy adjustments I might qualify for now that my marital status has changed?"

10. What other policies should I consider now that I'm divorced?

- ○ **Why it's essential:** Divorce might introduce the need for additional coverage, like long-term care insurance or more robust personal liability protection.
- ○ **How to ask:** "Given my new situation, are there any additional insurance policies you'd recommend to protect my assets and future?"

Remember, each divorce situation is unique, and these tips may not apply to every case. It's crucial to consult with professionals who can provide tailored advice based on your specific circumstances.

_____

_____

_____

_____

_____

_____

_____

_____

10 Essential Questions to Ask Your Retirement Specialist During Your Divorce

Divorce brings significant changes to every aspect of your life, and your retirement plans are no exception. Ensuring that your financial future remains secure requires careful planning, especially when dividing assets like 401(k)s, IRAs, or pensions. Working with a retirement specialist during your divorce can help you navigate the complexities of asset division, tax implications, and long-term financial planning. Asking the right questions is crucial to making informed decisions that will protect your retirement savings and provide stability for the years ahead. In this post, we'll explore 10 essential questions to discuss with your retirement specialist to help you prepare for a financially sound future after divorce.

---

1. How will my retirement accounts be divided in the divorce?

- **Why it's essential:** Understanding the rules for dividing retirement assets, such as 401(k)s, IRAs, and pensions, helps ensure that you receive your fair share and avoid costly mistakes. Some accounts require a Qualified Domestic Relations Order (QDRO) to divide funds.

- **How to ask:** "Can you explain how my retirement accounts will be divided and whether any require a QDRO or other legal steps?"

2. What are the tax implications of dividing retirement assets?

- ○ **Why it's essential:** Transferring retirement funds during divorce can have significant tax consequences if not handled properly. Knowing how to avoid penalties ensures you retain more of your assets.
- ○ **How to ask:** "What are the tax consequences of splitting my retirement accounts, and how can I minimize any penalties?"

3. Should I roll over retirement funds into a new account?

- ○ **Why it's essential:** Rolling over funds into a new account might protect them and offer better investment options, ensuring long-term growth.
- ○ **How to ask:** "Would it make sense for me to roll over retirement funds into a new account, and what options should I consider?"

4. How do I protect my retirement savings post-divorce?

- ○ **Why it's essential:** Divorce can deplete savings, but strategies like adjusting contributions and reassessing investment options can help rebuild your financial security.
- ○ **How to ask:** "What steps can I take to protect and rebuild my retirement savings after the divorce?"

5. How does divorce affect Social Security benefits?

- ○ **Why it's essential:** You might be entitled to spousal Social Security benefits if your marriage lasted 10 years or more, which could impact your financial planning.
- ○ **How to ask:** "Can you explain how my divorce might affect my eligibility for Social Security benefits, including spousal benefits?"

6. Do I need to update my retirement account beneficiaries?

- ○ **Why it's essential:** If your ex-spouse remains listed as a beneficiary, they might inherit your funds, potentially against your wishes.
- ○ **How to ask:** "How can I update my beneficiary designations on my retirement accounts to reflect my new circumstances?"

7. What impact does alimony or child support have on my retirement contributions?

- ○ **Why it's essential:** Changes in income due to alimony or child support payments can affect your ability to save for retirement.
- ○ **How to ask:** "How should I adjust my retirement contributions given the financial changes from alimony or child support?"

8. Are there penalties if I withdraw retirement funds early?

- ○ **Why it's essential:** If you need to access retirement funds during the divorce process, knowing the penalties and exceptions can help you avoid unnecessary financial losses.
- ○ **How to ask:** "What are the penalties for early withdrawal from my retirement accounts, and are there any exceptions I should know about?"

9. What role do pensions play in my divorce settlement?

- ○ **Why it's essential:** Pensions are often overlooked but can be valuable assets. Understanding how to value and divide them is crucial for a fair settlement.
- ○ **How to ask:** "How do pensions factor into my divorce settlement, and what should I know about their valuation and division?"

10. Should I revise my retirement timeline?

- ○ **Why it's essential:** Divorce may affect your retirement timeline by reducing savings or increasing financial obligations. A revised plan ensures you stay on track.
- ○ **How to ask:** "Given my divorce, do I need to reassess my retirement timeline, and how can I adjust my goals accordingly?"

By asking these targeted questions, you can work with your retirement specialist to safeguard your financial future and confidently navigate the complexities of divorce.

Remember, each divorce situation is unique, and these tips may not apply to every case. It's crucial to consult with professionals who can provide tailored advice based on your specific circumstances.

Find the Experts you need at freshstartsregistry.com/experts

10 Questions to Ask Your Estate Planner

Divorce can be an emotionally taxing process, filled with challenging decisions and complex legal matters. Amidst the emotional turmoil, it's easy to overlook the importance of estate planning during a divorce. However, consulting with an experienced estate lawyer can prove invaluable in ensuring your future financial security and protecting your assets. We rounded up 10 questions to ask your estate planner while going through a divorce - and why you should have these questions answered! By seeking professional guidance and understanding the intricacies of estate planning, you can empower yourself to make informed decisions that safeguard your interests and the well-being of your loved ones.

1. **Should I update my will and other estate planning documents?** Determine whether your existing will, trust, or other estate planning documents need to be revised or replaced to reflect your changing circumstances and wishes.

2. **How can I protect my assets during the divorce process? Seek advice on** implementing strategies to safeguard your assets during the divorce proceedings, such as establishing trusts or reevaluating beneficiary designations.

3. **Who should be the executor of my estate?** Discuss whether changes need to be made to the executor designation in your will, considering the impact of your divorce on your chosen executor and their ability to fulfill the role impartially.

4. **How should I address the division of assets in my estate plan?** Understand the implications of your divorce on asset distribution and discuss strategies to ensure that your intended beneficiaries receive their designated shares.

5. **Should I update my healthcare proxy or power of attorney?** Inquire about the need to update your healthcare proxy and power of attorney to reflect your current wishes, especially if your former spouse was previously designated.

6. **Who should be named as guardians for my children?** If you have minor children, discuss the selection of guardians and consider any changes necessitated by your divorce, ensuring that the chosen individuals are still suitable and willing to assume the responsibility.

7. **Can I establish a trust for my children's inheritance?** Explore the option of creating a trust to protect your children's inheritance, ensuring it is structured to align with your intentions and address any divorce-related concerns.

8. **How should I update beneficiary designations?** Review and update the beneficiaries listed on your life insurance policies, retirement accounts, and other assets to ensure they align with your current wishes and post-divorce arrangements.

9. **What impact does divorce have on my existing estate plan?** Understand how your divorce affects previously established provisions, such as spousal inheritance or distribution of assets, and discuss necessary modifications to reflect your new circumstances.

10. **Can you recommend any other professionals to consult during my divorce?** Seek referrals to other professionals, such as family law attorneys or financial advisors, who can provide expertise and guidance on specific divorce-related matters.

Remember, each divorce situation is unique, and these questions may not cover all aspects of your estate planning needs. It is essential to consult with an experienced estate planner who can provide tailored advice based on your specific circumstances.

Find the Experts you need at freshstartsregistry.com/experts

10 Essential Questions to Ask Your Bank and Credit Card Company During Your Divorce

Divorce is a major life transition, and managing your finances is one of the most critical aspects of navigating this change. From separating joint accounts to understanding how your credit score might be affected, having open and informed conversations with your bank and credit card company is essential to protecting your financial future. These institutions play a pivotal role in ensuring your financial independence, helping you avoid unnecessary pitfalls, and providing tools to rebuild stability.

In this post, we'll cover 10 essential questions to ask your bank and credit card company during your divorce. These questions will help you gain clarity on everything from account closures and debt responsibility to strategies for safeguarding your personal finances as you move forward.

1. What will happen to our joint accounts during the divorce?

- **Why it's essential:** Joint accounts need to be separated as part of the divorce process. Knowing how to split these accounts can avoid potential complications and unauthorized access.

- **How to ask:** "Can you walk me through the process of separating or closing our joint accounts and ensuring each party has access only to their individual accounts moving forward?"

2. Can I remove my ex-spouse from my accounts and credit cards

- ○ **Why it's essential:** If your spouse is still listed on your personal accounts or credit cards, it's important to remove them to protect yourself from liability

- ○ **How to ask:** "What steps do I need to take to remove my ex-spouse from all accounts and ensure that they no longer have access to my financial information?"

3. How will divorce impact my credit score and reporting?

- ○ **Why it's essential:** Divorce can affect your credit score if joint debts are not properly divided or if your spouse fails to make payments. Understanding how to protect your credit is crucial.

- ○ **How to ask:** "Can you provide information about how divorce may affect my credit score, and what steps I can take to maintain my credit rating during this process?"

4. How can I close or freeze joint credit cards?

- ○ **Why it's essential:** Closing or freezing joint credit cards can prevent further debt accumulation and financial surprises.

- ○ **How to ask:** "What is the process for closing or freezing joint credit cards, and how can I ensure that I'm not liable for any charges made after the divorce?"

5. Will I be responsible for any shared debt post-divorce?

- ○ **Why it's essential:** Understanding your financial obligations is crucial, as divorce doesn't automatically erase joint debt. You'll need to clarify who is responsible for which debts.

- ○ **How to ask:** "How can I ensure that shared debt is properly assigned during the divorce, and what will happen if my ex-spouse fails to make their portion of the payments?"

6. **How can I protect my individual assets, such as savings accounts or investments, from my spouse's access?**

   ○ **Why it's essential:** Divorce can affect ownership of assets. Protecting your personal accounts and investments is key to ensuring your financial independence.

   ○ **How to ask:** "Can you advise on steps to protect my personal assets and accounts from my spouse's access during the divorce proceedings?"

7. **What happens if my ex-spouse and I have a joint mortgage?**

   ○ **Why it's essential:** A joint mortgage needs to be handled carefully to ensure you're not left with an unwanted financial responsibility after divorce.

   ○ **How to ask:** "What options are available for managing a joint mortgage, and what are the implications for my credit and finances if my ex-spouse remains on the mortgage post-divorce?"

8. **How can I ensure that my name is removed from any loans or credit cards taken out during our marriage?**

   ○ **Why it's essential:** If your ex-spouse has taken out loans or credit cards in both of your names, it's important to ensure you're no longer financially liable for them.

   ○ **How to ask:** "How can I verify that I'm no longer listed as a co-signer or responsible party for any loans or credit cards taken out during the marriage?"

9. **How do I set up individual bank accounts and transition to separate financial systems?**

   ◦ **Why it's essential:** Establishing your financial independence is crucial during and after divorce. Setting up separate accounts will ensure you have control over your money.

   ◦ **How to ask:** "Can you help me with setting up my own accounts, and what's the process for ensuring that all future deposits and transactions are separate from my ex-spouse?"

10. **How will my divorce impact my eligibility for joint benefits (health insurance, retirement accounts, etc.)?**

    ◦ **Why it's essential:** If you've been on your spouse's health insurance or retirement plan, divorce may affect your eligibility for these benefits.

    ◦ **How to ask:** "Can you explain how divorce will affect my eligibility for joint benefits like health insurance, retirement plans, or other financial services?"

By asking these crucial questions, you can navigate the financial complexities of divorce more effectively. Don't hesitate to consult with experts such as financial planners, divorce attorneys, or credit counselors who can offer additional guidance on managing your finances through this transition. Getting the right answers now will help you regain control over your financial future and set you up for success after divorce.

Remember, each divorce situation is unique, and these tips may not apply to every case. It's crucial to consult with professionals who can provide tailored advice based on your specific circumstances.

Thank you for taking the time to read Your Divorce Support Team.

We understand that navigating divorce can be incredibly challenging, and Fresh Starts Registry is here to support you every step of the way.

Visit freshstartsregistry.com for:

- *Access to vetted Divorce Experts*

- *Free Divorce Consultations*

- *Supportive Resource Guides*

- *Emotional and practical checklists to help you through every stage*

Schedule your free 15-minute divorce consultation to get started on your journey to empowerment and clarity.

You are not alone—Fresh Starts Registry is here to guide you to your new beginning.

Let's build your fresh start together.